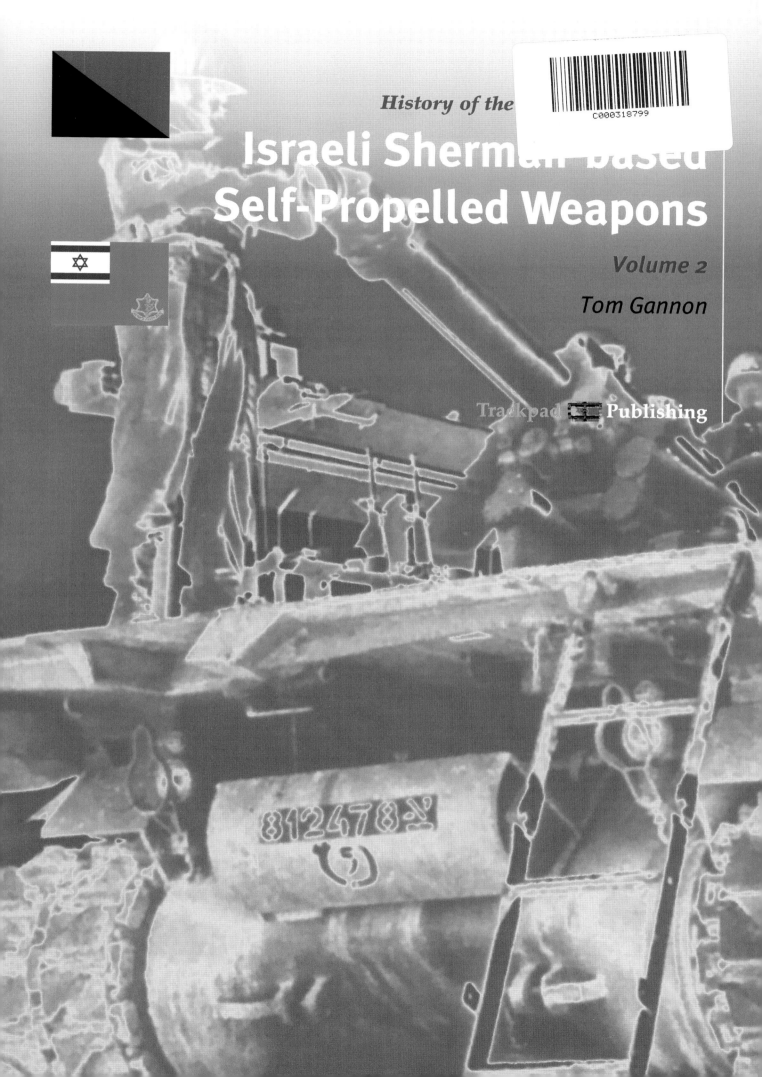

History of the

Israeli Sherman-based
Self-Propelled Weapons

Volume 2

Tom Gannon

Trackpad Publishing

"God fights on the side with the best artillery."
(Napoleon Bonaparte)

"Without support, the infantry won't move!"
(IDF Artillery Corps motto)

LANGUAGE
Due to the author's American origin, American spelling has been used in this book.

PHOTOGRAPHS
Some of the photographs in this volume are not of the best quality. There is a scarcity of in-service photos to be found through normal archival sources and personal contributions. Due to their rarity and historical value, and their importance in telling the full story, it was felt important to include them.

COVER CAPTIONS
Front Cover: All new IDF weapon systems and vehicles are presented at exhibitions, always for government and military officials, and sometimes for the general public. This *Ro'em Degem Alef* is displayed along with its contents and crew, at one of these exhibitions. Note that in this case at least, the uniforms are one-piece overalls with American-type webbing and American 'bone-dome' AFV (**A**rmored **F**ighting **V**ehicle) helmets. This innovative vehicle is described, in detail, in Chapter 2. (Defense Establishment Archives)

Back Cover 1: The main entrance to *Beit Ha'Totchan* features what is said to be the former home of a member of one of the town's founding families. The displays include prototypes, test subjects and weapons and vehicles retired from service. The L33 *Ro'em*, in the foreground, is described in detail in Chapter 7. To the left, in the photo, is a test vehicle from the shared US Army/IDF HIP (**H**owitzer **I**mprovement **P**rogram) program, which ultimately led to the development of the M109A6 Paladin, while the last vehicle is one of the *Merkava*-based 155mm *Sho'lef* self-propelled howitzers. Neither of these last two vehicles saw active Artillery Corps service.

Back Cover 2: The exhibits at *Beit Ha'Totchan* are placed along dirt paths that wind through the trees, making for a very tranquil setting. The buildings in the background are in the town itself.

Back Cover 3: The Hatzerim Air Base is located in the Negev Desert near Be'er Sheva. Public access is restricted to the museum only. The *Kilshon* shown here is described in detail in Chapter 9.

 Israeli Artillery Corps Insignia

 Israeli Defence Forces Flag

Contents

The Author

Born in January, 1949, the author grew up near Baltimore, Maryland in the United States of America. A business credit manager by profession, his hobby interests include armor modeling and researching Sherman tanks and the Israeli Defense Forces. He is a regular visitor to various Internet armor discussion forums, and has presented seminars on armor subjects at model shows in the US.

He is married to the love of his life, Connie Baker. Between them, they have four children and five grandchildren:
Bryan Gannon
Heather (Gannon) Eyler, married to Herb, with granddaughter, Julia
Melissa Baker, with granddaughters, Cora and
Charlie Ann
Justin Baker, married to Laurie, with grandsons, Dylan and Reid

Previous works include:
Israeli Sherman, Tracing the History of the Sherman Tank in Israeli Service, 2001
Israeli Half-tracks, Volumes One and Two, 2008
Israeli Sherman, Second Edition, 2017

This photo was taken at *Yad La'Shiryon*, during the 2005 Memorial Day week celebrations and commemorations.
From left to right: Alex von Reizen and Jan-Willem de Boer (Netherlands), Joshua Weingarten (USA), David 'Didi' Levy (Israel), me, Michael Mass (Israel, Curator at the Latrun museum)

Introduction

As shown in Volume 1, the IDF made good use of some proven vehicle types, with the Priest and its development of the *TOMAT* M50 155mm howitzer, the design of which was similar to that of several World War II weapons.

As we continue the study of *Heil Ha'Totchan's* use of the Sherman tank as a basis for artillery, we will see some creativity and innovation with new designs. These weapons, both tube artillery and rocket launchers, continued in IDF use into the 1980s and 1990s.

There were also a few other vehicle types that also show some interesting adaptions of the ubiquitous Sherman for other uses.

Vehicles covered in this volume include: *MACHMAT* 160mm SP mortar, L33 *Ro'em* 155mm SP howitzer, MAR 240 & MAR 290 rocket launchers, *Kilshon* rocket launcher, *Eyal* Observation Post Tank, Medical Evacuation Tank, Driver Trainer and the M10 Tank Destroyer.

IDF artillery is prominently featured at several locations in Israel:

Beit Ha'Totchan (Gunners' House) is a memorial and museum dedicated to the fallen members of *Heil Ha'Totchanim* (IDF Artillery Corps). It is located in the picturesque northern town of Zichron Ya'akov, close to the coast. The main building is surrounded by acres of trees and paths, along which one can see exhibits depicting many of the towed and self-propelled artillery pieces used over the years. In a plaza in front of the main building, are stone pillars bearing the names of 756 fallen artillerymen.

The **Israeli Air Force Museum** is located on the grounds of Hatzerim Air Base, southwest of Be'er Sheva, seen here in the background, in the Negev Desert. Its focus is, of course, on the many types of aircraft used by the IAF. Among its varied exhibits are a Spitfire, a P-51 Mustang, several *Kfirs* and the Boeing 707 that was used as a flying command post during the famous Entebbe rescue mission. For our purposes here, there are also vehicles and anti-aircraft artillery used by the IAF. Interestingly enough, during my 1999 visit, the female airman at the ticket window was a reservist, whose family residence was in Silver Spring, MD, in the US, and she attended my *alma mater*, the University of Maryland.

Soltam Systems Ltd. produced the 160mm Heavy Mortar M66. Based on a Finnish design, this impressive weapon fired an 85-pound (38.5 kilogram) high-explosive round out to a range of approximately six miles (9,600 meters). The M66 required a crew of six to eight men. This mortar is shown being prepared for a firing mission during the 1960s. At the beginning of the Six-Day War, the IDF had a single battalion in service with these powerful mortars, drawn by half-tracks. This weapon differed from a standard mortar in that it lacked a normal bipod. (Israeli Government Press Office)

TOWED *MACHMAT* 160MM MORTAR

Several countries had experimented with the idea of mounting heavy mortars in vehicles, with varied degrees of success. For instance, as early as 1942, the United States Army had begun testing at Aberdeen Proving Ground to determine if a 4.2-inch (106.7mm) mortar could be successfully installed in half-tracks. Subsequent trials with the mortar mounted to fire either forward or to the rear in a modified Mortar Motor Carriage M4 failed, due to the stress placed on the vehicle's structure, even with thick rubber matting under the base plate. A second trial vehicle, designated T21, based on a mortar firing to the rear in an M3A1 half-track, complete with machine gun pulpit, also failed. It was only after a third attempt using an M3A1, minus the pulpit and designated T21E1, with a reinforced frame and a mortar set to fire forward, that there was some success.

This 160mm mortar is about to be fired. The size of the round is evident, because of the loading rack. Also note the firing position of the carriage. (IDF Encyclopedia)

This was the Soltam Systems, Ltd. Plant in Yokneam in 1967, around the time the M66 was introduced. The first photo shows a worker transferring 160mm mortar tubes to the assembly line. In the second picture, another worker inspects a completed M66 in the same factory. Both images clearly show the massive size of this mortar. (Ilan Bruner, Israeli Government Press Office)

However, American interest in a half-track mortar carrier waned and the project was terminated. The main issue was the powerful recoil from a mortar of this size – and the relative weakness of the half-track chassis. When the IDF decided to mount an even more powerful 120mm mortar, designers accounted for the recoil by building the mortar base into the frame itself. The reinforced structure was a success and the M3 *Degem Dalet* (Type D) served from the early 1960s to the 1980s and beyond.

Towards the end of 1962, design work began on the idea for an even heavier self-propelled mortar. Under the direction of Ordnance Corps Captain (later Lieutenant Colonel) Zvi Orbach, the design team tested several varieties of towed mortars, looking at rates of fire, accuracy, blast effect, range and mobility. Their final choice was a 160mm design from Tampella in Finland, to be manufactured under license in Israel by Soltam Systems, Ltd. Mortars of this caliber and their associated size and weight were/are not used at all, much less in a mobile role, by very many countries. Consequently, there was no similar experience from which to draw. Israeli Ordnance would have to do it all from scratch. In addition to its mobile role, the 160mm mortar was also used in the ground mode, usually towed behind a half-track.

Unlike with a lighter weapon, the M66 requires four wheels in the towing mode. Due to its size, and the weight of its projectile, the tube was lowered for loading, and raised back up to fire. This was accomplished using the single hydraulic tube at the front and the wire cables to the rear. In the background, friends of the author include, from the left, Alex van Riezen from the Netherlands, David 'Didi' Levy from Israel, and Joshua Weingarten from the USA.

MACHMAT 160ᴍᴍ (Iɴ Sᴇʀᴠɪᴄᴇ)

Once again, Israeli Ordnance considered its already extensive experience with the Sherman when deciding how to deal with such a massive weapon. Creative design work was required to allow for the large size of the weapon itself, the crew needed to serve it, its ammunition storage, not to mention the tremendous recoil. Using its prior experience with the half-track-mounted 120mm mortars, Israeli Ordnance proceeded along a similar path. The solution, in both cases, was to incorporate the mortar mount into the basic vehicle structure, allowing the vehicle's suspension to absorb the recoil. As with the previous *TOMAT* M50 155mm, the intention was to use both M4A4s (Sherman V) and short-hull Shermans lengthened to M4A4 standards.

From the beginning, the design included the Cummins VT8-460 diesel engine and HVSS (**H**orizontal **V**olute **S**pring **S**uspension). The resultant vehicle was designated the *MACHMAT* 160mm. In this case, the extension insert was incorporated farther forward, below the mortar mount, for added strength as part of the overall effort to transmit the recoil to the suspension. The front weld seam bisected the first large return roller mount, compared to the rear one on the *TOMAT* M50. Even with the long hull as standard, the area needed to install and serve the massive mortar was so large that the engine compartment still required the same 4-inch (10cm) door extension on the lower rear plate, as used on the regular short-hull Sherman gun tanks.

MACHMAT is a Hebrew acronym for 'self-propelled heavy mortar', pronounced as a single word. The term also refers to the 120mm series, mounted in half-tracks. (Translation provided by an IDF Artillery Corps veteran.)

M is the Hebrew letter *Mem*. In this case it is short for **M**argema = mortar.

A is the Hebrew letter *Aleph*, included for pronunciation purposes.

CH stands in for the Hebrew letter *Kaf* which is part of the word **K**veda = heavy.

MAT comes from the word **M**i**T**naya'at = self-propelled.

(In many languages, certain words are differentiated by gender, as in French and Hebrew amongst others. In this case 'gun' is male, while 'mortar' is female, thus the different words designating 'self-propelled'.)

At first glance, the vehicle looks boxy and primitive until one understands and appreciates the functionality and efficiency incorporated into it. The large fighting compartment was open-topped, with flat sides tilted inward at the top. This box structure extended from the front edge of the standard Cummins engine deck forward, to a point just above and behind the transmission cover. The front plate could be lowered and raised hydraulically to allow more room for loading the mortar. When in the firing position, the standard Sherman driver's station, which was now inside the box, was covered by hinged floor plates. Similar plates

This *MACHMAT* 160mm is shown during the introduction ceremony at Yokneam, in 1969. This excellent right-side view shows a complete set of equipment stowage. At the rear is one of the large ammunition lockers. Also, the large assembly at the top of the front corner was for a .50-caliber Browning M2 HB (**H**eavy **B**arrel) machine gun. (Defense Establishment Archives)

on the other side, gave access to ammunition storage. Ready rounds, in tubes, were stowed in upright rows, along both sides. Four seats were attached to the rear wall. Two large ammunition storage bins flanked the engine deck, taking the place of the normal Sherman sponson fuel tanks. Total onboard ammunition capacity was a hefty 55 rounds.

Other enhancements included installing a hydraulic system to assist with lowering the mortar tube, because the weapon was a standard muzzle loader. The ammunition racks were designed to slide along the side, allowing for the next ready round to be at the front. However, this functionality was not evident in the three vehicles presently on display, suggesting that the feature was not incorporated into production vehicles.

The mortar itself, designated the M66, was derived from Tampella's (Finland) M58 mortar, and built under license by Soltam. Serviced by a crew of six to eight men, it fired an 85-pound (38.5 kilogram) HE (**H**igh-**E**xplosive) round very accurately out to 10,600 yards (9,601 meters). The barrel was a high-tensile-strength steel alloy tube with the firing mechanism in the breech. This firing mechanism could be removed, for safety reasons if necessary. It was elevated and depressed by a single hydraulic column in the front

and two cables at the rear, all of which were part of the mount itself. It was manually traversed through the frontal arc, using a hand wheel attached to the vehicle floor. Given the weight of the round that had to be fed down the muzzle, the crews' average rate of fire of five rounds per minute was rather impressive. To assist with loading, the elevating strut was hinged to allow the tube to be lowered, and then to be raised again to its original position, using a spring-loaded counter-balance mechanism. Some tubes were later fitted with a cylindrical muzzle brake, but this does not appear to be universal. The sights were the same as used on the 120mm series.

Production took place at *BMB*-681 (Hebrew letters *Bet Mem Bet* to indicate the concept of Base Workshop, as in the British acronym BWS for **B**ase **W**ork**s**hop). First, if the hull being used was not originally from an M4A4, it had to be cut and lengthened with the appropriate changes made to accommodate the HVSS suspension. Because of the size of the fighting compartment and the space taken by incorporating the massive mortar base into the hull itself, the engine compartment required some changes, as mentioned earlier.

Firing tests were first conducted in the Arava Valley, between the Dead Sea and the Red Sea, and later along the coast, near Rishon Lezion. Rishon Lezion, south of

Tel-Aviv, was founded in 1882. It was the site of the second Jewish settlement in Israel, after Petach Tikva, founded in 1878. Mobility tests took place in the Negev Desert in a place known as Nachal Zin.

Design and development work ended in June 1966, but the Six-Day War delayed the project somewhat. Consequently, the first 15 production vehicles were not fielded until 1968. The first unit so equipped was 334 Battalion, assigned to the *Golani* Brigade, as replacements for its *MACHMAT* 120mm half-tracks. In recognition of the extensive and innovative design work on this weapon system, the design team was awarded Israel's highest decoration for military developments in June 1969.

The first operational use of the *MACHMAT* 160mm was along the Suez Canal, during the War of Attrition. It remained in service for a number of years, being heavily used in the *Yom Kippur* War. At that time, the IDF was woefully deficient in night-fighting equipment so, in addition to normal fire support, the *MACHMAT* 160mm was often used to provide illumination at night.

At the start of Operation Peace for Galilee in Lebanon in 1982, there were apparently six battalions still operational. They accounted for a significant percentage of all artillery fire support in Northern Command. According to another Israeli friend, it was actually an IDF *MACHMAT* 160mm unit – his – that fired the last shot of this long Lebanon campaign in 2000.

At the same introduction exhibition, this vehicle was set up to display its basic contents, with an open view of the interior. The large front plate served a dual role as the platform for the crew to load and fire the mortar. More details of the interior are to be seen in the color photos. (Defense Establishment Archives)

As late as 1999, while driving to the IAF Museum at Hatzerim, near Be'er Sheva, the author observed a weathered vehicle on a transporter returning from training exercises in the Negev. Knowing the prohibition against photographing active IDF units or bases, and given the presence of a number of soldiers, no pictures were taken, sadly. Around the same general timeframe, only months before its demise, the SLA (**S**outh **L**ebanon **A**rmy) received a small number of reconditioned *MACHMAT* 160mm vehicles (12 according to a Lebanese source). When the SLA finally did collapse, and the IDF withdrew in 2000, the IAF apparently found itself having to destroy at least three of these vehicles with air-to-ground rocket fire to keep them from being commandeered by *Hezbollah*. At least one other was photographed by the media being paraded around with *Hezbollah* flags, as were various other former SLA vehicles and weapons. Two others were recovered by the Lebanese Army and are in outside storage.

11

The photo above could be the same vehicle as shown on page 10, as it was driven during the 1969 ceremony. The second picture shows one vehicle of an entire unit of *MACHMAT* 160s passing in review, at the close of the ceremony. Note that these vehicles were more fully stowed with, for instance, the fire extinguishers and machine gun in place. (Defense Establishment Archives)

This is obviously a training exercise rather than combat, given the rather jovial attitude of the crew in the first photo. This was, however, a typical picture of how the vehicle, its ammunition and the crew, would have appeared in combat. The second photo provides a mostly unobstructed view of the interior as the vehicle underwent an inspection. (Defense Establishment Archives)

During an Artillery Corps officers' graduation ceremony, this fully-crewed *MACHMAT* 160mm passes the crowd and the reviewing stand (unseen). Note that a number of fittings are painted in a dark color, likely black, although red was also an option. Usually, the colors indicated items that required maintenance, but they could be used for ceremonial purposes. (Israeli Government Press Office)

A *MACHMAT* 160mm of 334 Battalion poised and ready on the border with Jordan during the War of Attrition in 1970. The location is opposite the destroyed Naharayim electric power plant, the first to be built in old Palestine. The two spare wheels on the rear plate are an unusual feature. Note the cover over the ready rounds along the side, of which there is no indication on the various museum display vehicles. (Yossi Ran, 334 Battalion Album, via Itamar Rotlevi)

As part of its rotation to the front along the Canal, 334 Battalion was in action opposite Ismailia in 1970. Judging by the number of rounds and empty containers, the firing was sustained for some time. (Yossi Ran, 334 Battalion Album, via Itamar Rotlevi)

334 Battalion was posted near *Kibbutz* Tel Katzir, below the Golan Heights, following the War of Attrition. The crew's demeanor may be light and jovial but the presence of 24–25 rounds stacked in front of the mortar would seem to indicate the possibility of action or, at the very least, an extended period of training. The visible ammo would have been in addition to the stored rounds along the right side of the interior. Note the coloring on the rounds. (Yossi Ran, 334 Battalion Album, via Itamar Rotlevi)

This crew from 334 Battalion is seen resting during training in the desert. The training mode is confirmed by the covered machine gun. (Yossi Ran, 334 Battalion Album, via Itamar Rotlevi)

Here is another resting crew during a training exercise. This time it was in an area with some vegetation. The crew are listening to a commercial radio, seen sitting on top of a mortar round. The propellant disks were covered in plastic, including the one still partly in its storage tube. Note the soldier sitting on the mortar, also shown as part of a *TOMAT* M50 crew (see Volume 1), as well as in some *MACHMAT* 120mm half-tracks in other photos (not shown). (Yossi Ran, 334 Battalion Album, via Itamar Rotlevi)

These crewmen are seen resting in the shade, on October 14, 1973. This was the date of the massive, yet unsuccessful, Egyptian attack which preceded the Israeli counter-attack the following day. Given the relaxed posture of these men, the Egyptians have already been stopped. The vehicle is ready for action, however, with the loading ramp in its lowered position, and a full ammo belt for the Browning M2 HB. (Israeli Government Press Office)

This *MACHMAT* 160mm is in position where its unit is widely dispersed in the Sinai, during the *Yom Kippur* War. The unit is unknown, as is the original source of the photo, but it is presumed to have been taken by an Artillery Corps veteran, given its quality. It gives an indication of the vastness of that battlefield. An interesting feature is that the mortar tube has a muzzle brake attached. Note also, the framing for a sunscreen, not yet raised.

There is no doubt, however, that this photograph depicts a vehicle in a combat situation. The location is the Golan Heights. Note the number of empty mortar round containers, including one that was haphazardly dropped onto the engine deck where it rests against the door protecting the sponson fuel filler cap. (IDF Spokesman via Michael Mass)

The mortar round itself weighed 85 pounds (38.5 kilograms). For loading, the tube was lowered to provide easier access. In the first photograph, the loaders are ready as the tube is lowered. In the second shot, they are about to slide the round down the tube. It will then be raised back up to fire. Note the ammunition containers on the ground, even as the racks on board appear to be full. (Defense Establishment Archives)

Another round is about to be dropped down the mortar tube as this crew prepares for the substantial blast, not normally associated with smaller mortars. (Defense Establishment Archives)

This alert crew is part of a column advancing along the Golan. The machine gunner is ready, while others go through other preparations. The soldier on the right keeps his eyes ahead, as does the driver. (Defense Establishment Archives)

A number of IDF vehicles, seen here in 1973 in what is apparently a staging area, away from the combat zone. The photograph is undated. Note the *MACHMAT* 160mm and the Priest together. Even with all of the war activity around her, a young *kibbutznik* goes about her regular chores. (Defense Establishment Archives)

The strange looking object jutting out from the top – seen from a distance in the previous photograph – is the ladder attached to the front plate. The mortar tube was covered against dust and the weather. The location was near one of the settlements on the Golan Heights. (Defense Establishment Archives)

This column is moving along but in the Sinai theater of operations this time. The crew also looks to be a little more jovial, perhaps indicating a successful action or, better still, the beginning of the trip home. (Defense Establishment Archives)

This vehicle is definitely beyond any threat of immediate action with the machine gun covered. The location was the Golan Heights. The angle of the photo provides an excellent view of the long hull. (Defense Establishment Archives)

The *MACHMAT* 160mm shown here was at a field maintenance depot somewhere on the Golan Heights. Note the *Sho't* (IDF-upgraded Centurion) to the right and the boom of an M32 ARV behind it. The crane backed up to it may be about to pull its engine. (Defense Establishment Archives)

The 1973 Independence Day parade was the last of its type. However, that did not stop the IDF from putting on a victory parade following the Yom Kippur War. This *MACHMAT* 160mm carrier participated in that parade in Jerusalem. The vehicle was fully outfitted, including what looks like a Browning .30-caliber machine gun in place of the usual M2 HB. Note the US-style tanker helmets, popularly known as the 'bone-dome'.

This *MACHMAT* 16omm battery was near the Syrian village of Hader in January 1974. The front plates are lowered. However, since the truce was in effect, there does not seem to be any other indication that any kind of action was imminent. The inverted 'V' is the battery indicator, with guns one and two shown in the photograph. (Asher Dank, Artillery Corps veteran, via Itamar Rotlevi)

This religious soldier is in the middle of his prayers, not far from his *MACHMAT* 16omm. Note the partially-raised frame for the weather tarp, as well as the full elevation of the mortar. He is diligent in his religious responsibilities, as part of a crew that is equally diligent in being prepared for possible action. (Defense Establishment Archives)

The muzzle flash has illuminated this mortar during night firing. Note the cover over the ready rounds. Again, this does not seem to be long-lived, since it does not appear on any of the vehicles shown in the following section. (Yossi Ran, 334 Battalion Album, via Itamar Rotlevi)

In this photograph, the flash is so intense that it has lit up the markings on the vehicle. These last two photographs were taken during training exercises. (Yossi Ran, 334 Battalion Album, via Itamar Rotlevi)

The *MACHMAT* 160mm was heavily used in Lebanon, right up to the withdrawal in 2000. One of these mortars fired the final shot of the campaign. This tired crew is resting after what must be some extended firing, given the heat effects on the mortar tube itself. (Claude Benshaul, Artillery Corps veteran)

UNIFIL (**U**nited **N**ations **I**nterim **F**orce **in** **L**ebanon) forces stand by, as an IDF *MACHMAT* 160mm mortar battalion leaves Lebanon.

This photo of a wreck in Lebanon, even in this condition, is an excellent opportunity to see the inside weld seam where the hull extension was added. The cause of the destruction appears to be from below the vehicle. Of course it could also be from a through-and-through hit from an armor-piercing air-to-ground rocket that exploded beneath the vehicle. Therefore, this may be one of the SLA vehicles destroyed by the IAF.

The *MACHMAT* 160mm conversion on the Sherman was a highly successful innovation. Consequently, it remained in service for a long time. This photograph was taken in 2004, and yet the vehicle seems ready to move at a moment's notice. Its paint is pristine, and the placards and hoses are intact and devoid of any paint. It is also painted in the modern IDF olive drab that would eventually fade to a grayish olive color. The mortar tube is also still being protected against dust and the weather. (Michael Mass)

Yad La'Shiryon, 2005: When in action, the front plate was lowered to allow room for loading the large, but otherwise standard, mortar. Rubber-tipped feet rest on the specially-designed fenders. The heavy plate was lowered and raised hydraulically, as indicated by the cylinders on the side, just above and behind the hinges.

Yad La'Shiryon, 2005: The design for this weapon system was so dramatically different – the only recognizable original Sherman components were the suspension and drive train. From this angle, the standard Cummins engine deck is visible. Unlike the *TOMAT* M50 155mm conversions and the M-50/M-51 gun tanks, the *MACHMAT* 160mm was designed, from its inception, around the Cummins and the HVSS suspension. Consequently, the vehicles' appearance changed little over the years.

Yad La'Shiryon, 2005: Even though all *MACHMAT* 160mm mortar carriers were built on a long hull, it still required the rear door extension common to short-hull Cummins vehicles. The two ladders fold up, secured with the clips visible above the top permanent step. This conversion was done on a vehicle not previously used as a Cummins-equipped tank, thus the lack of a covered exhaust port to the left of the rear doors.

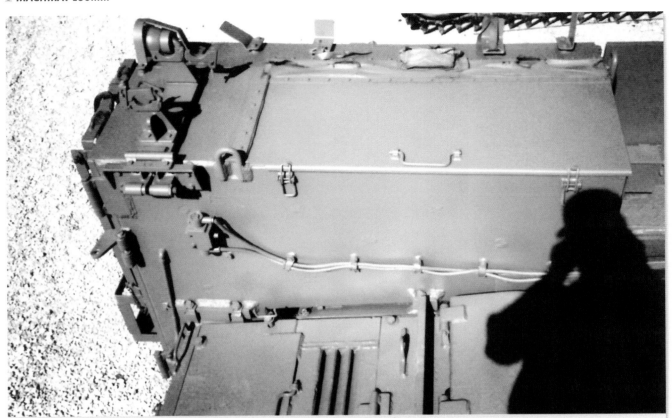

Yad La'Shiryon: From 1999, this photograph was taken just after the vehicle was freshly painted in the modern IDF grayish olive drab. This was the left-side ammunition stowage bin. It opened at the top, the rear and the side, giving ready access to the rounds. Note the cabling which would connect the vehicle's communication system to a cable reel, the bracket for which is shown here. This, in turn, would connect to a network for the battery fire control officer. It folded over the inside edge, out of the way, when necessary.

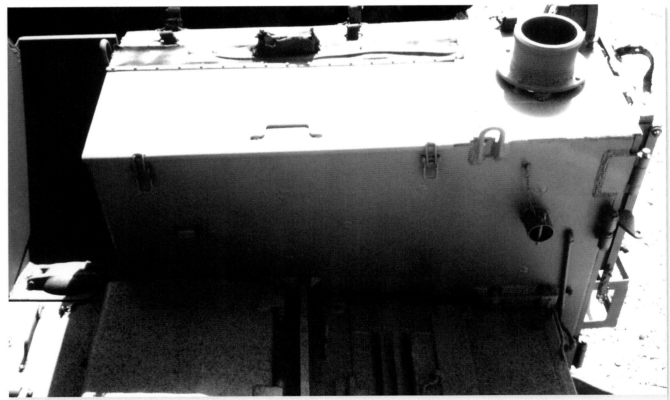

Yad La'Shiryon, 1999: The right-side bin was nearly a mirror image of the other. The purpose of the cylindrical object is not known, at the time of this writing. The only visible cabling inside was for the rear lamp. Note that the track-tensioning wrench would be stowed on the side.

Batey Haosef, 2005: For some time, this *MACHMAT* 160mm was the only one on public display. As such, it caused some confusion about the appearance of these unique vehicles. In fact, it was a test bed for another mortar, as well as a new engine. The weapon seen here was not the standard tube used on operational vehicles. Note also the non-standard ID number applied, using weld bead. All other surviving vehicles appear to have the standard, post-1973, welded-on plate.

Batey Haosef, 2005: This is a very clear view of the lower door extension, minus the doors and hinges. There is no plated-over exhaust port in this case, either. Note the angular appearance of the lower edge on the hull. M4A4s were built with a rounded contour here so, even without seeing the welds on the sides, this confirms that this was originally a short hull.

29

Yad La'Shiryon, 2005: Conversions were done on both the M4A4 (Sherman V) and short-hull Shermans. However, unlike the *TOMAT* M50, the insert was placed toward the front of the vehicle. The front weld seam, visible here in the original image of the Latrun exhibit, bisected the first large return roller assembly. The rear seam can just be seen, behind the center suspension bogie. Note the beveled edges on the hull bottom, next to each wheel location. This was done to permit wheel changes without removing the entire unit. Factory work was neater than many retrofits, so the crisp edges may mean that this hull was originally equipped with HVSS, as built. (Joshua Weingarten)

Batey Haosef, 2005: As with the Latrun vehicle, there is a prominent weld seam running vertically below the first large return roller, also visible in the image above.

Batey Haosef, 2005: Although this was not the standard mortar, this photograph clearly shows the massive base that was incorporated into the hull to provide stability for the significant recoil force generated when fired. Note the folding doors over the driver station.

Batey Haosef, 2005: From the front, the nature of the base, and its integration into the hull, is a little more evident. (Eran Kaufman)

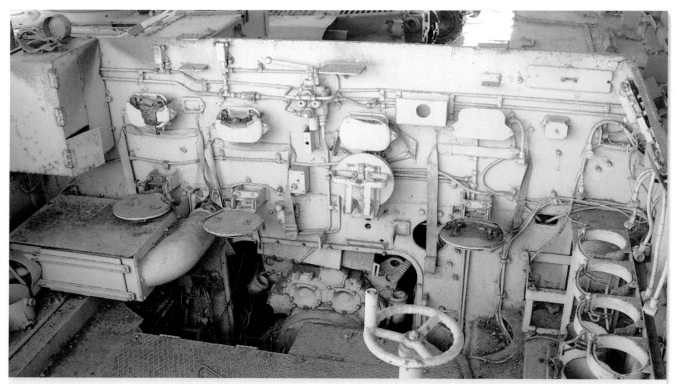

Batey Haosef, 2005: As mentioned, this vehicle was a test-bed for a new weapon, and a new engine. Here, the open firewall shows a General Motors diesel engine installed for this testing. The air cleaner, to the top left, is not standard either, as will be evident in some later photos. (Eran Kaufman)

Batey Haosef, 2005: This engine deck layout is nearly identical to that of the modified M-50 tanks sold to Chile in the 1980s. Whether this installation was solely for the purpose of that export sale, those tanks are equipped with this new General Motors diesel. Note the fuel filler cap between the rear wall and the storage box. This, and a corresponding section on the other side, were the only parts of the original upper-hull that were left. The ammunition storage boxes extend down to what would be the sponson floor level. However, they were not an actual part of the original hull, again, as will be seen later.

The third museum display is at *Beit Ha'Hotchan*. Although the paint is in poor shape it is in otherwise good condition. In contrast with the other two display vehicles, the front plate is in the lowered position. There are also some detail differences between vehicles. This, and the next 33 photographs, provide an excellent source of all-around detail information. The two hooks on the corners of the front plate were used to secure it when it was in the raised position.

Beit Ha'Totchan, 2005: Compare this round to the three in the two previous photographs. All are labeled with the same lot number. This one is complete, including the colored disks that contain the propellant. While this is a high-explosive round, the mortar also fired colored smoke and white phosphorous rounds at a rate of five per minute. Given the weight of the projectile, 85 pounds (38.5 kilograms), this is an impressive rate of fire. (Itamar Rotlevi)

Beit Ha'Hotchan, 2005: The projectiles are displayed on a rectangular plate that was not part of the vehicle itself. At one time, there was a fourth round, as indicated by the odd post on the right. The locking hook is very apparent in this view.

Beit Ha'Totchan, 2005: Although it is not visible in this image, this vehicle had the insert used to lengthen a standard hull to M4A4 standards. As with the Latrun vehicle, the forward weld seam bisected the large front return roller. Note that location of the insert, compared to the mortar base. Through innovative engineering, the entire vehicle suspension acted as a base to absorb the recoil. The bins along the track run were used to store a variety of items, just as with the *TOMAT* M50, although these are not labeled. Some of them are quite deep.

Beit Ha'Totchan, 2005: In this rear view, it is clear that the side boxes were attached to, but not part of the vehicle structure. Note the gap between them and the hull. The small ladders are missing in this case. Note that the idler mounts for the HVSS suspension were asymmetrical, which is often overlooked. (Itamar Rotlevi)

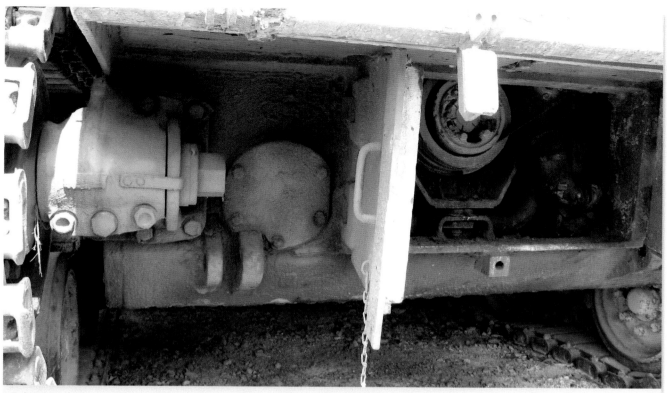

Beit Ha'Totchan, 2005: The single round and plated-over exhaust port indicates that this conversion was done using a tank hull, already previously fitted with the Cummins diesel engine. It may have been an unserviceable gun tank, or the rear plate may have been cannibalized from a battle casualty. One close look at the rear engine mount and it is very clear why the extension was needed. The brace was attached to the door frame itself.

Beit Ha'Totchan, 2005: The next series of photographs provides an all-around look at the complex interior. Beginning with the right front, this is part of the mechanism used to lower and raise the heavy front plate.

Beit Ha'Totchan, 2005: Eight photographs show details of the mortar. First, the mortar was traversed in a limited arc along the curved plate on the deck. Elevation was by means of the hydraulic post in the center, assisted by cables on either side.

Ha'Totchan, 2005: The vertical post and wheel was for traverse, and the others handle elevation.

Beit Ha'Totchan, 2005: The muzzle brake was introduced later in service, and it does not seem to have been universally installed.

Beit Ha'Totchan, 2005: This is the mortar from the rear, showing details of the mount.

Beit Ha'Totchan, 2005: This is the center pivot arm between and below the hydraulic cylinders. (Joshua Weingarten)

Beit Ha'Totchan, 2005: These three photographs provide details of the rear of the mortar, as well as part of the traverse mechanism. Note that the handles and wheels bear traces of the red paint used to enhance visibility.

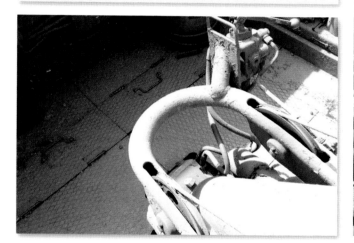

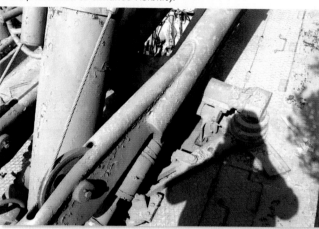

37

Beit Ha'Totchan, 2005: Mortar rounds were stowed along both sides, in the large rear bins and under the floor in the former co-driver compartment. Ten rounds were stored along the right side. There is a swivel mount for a .50 caliber machine gun forward and a socket for an additional machine gun, farther back. Note the red handle, at the top left. This engages the hook on the front plate, securing it the closed position. There is another, on the vehicle's left-side.

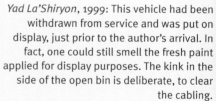

Beit Ha'Totchan, 2005: At the rear were racks for five rifles, including one that did not fit, on the raised side platform. Note the method for storing the mortar round in its fiber-board tube.

Yad La'Shiryon, 1999: This vehicle had been withdrawn from service and was put on display, just prior to the author's arrival. In fact, one could still smell the fresh paint applied for display purposes. The kink in the side of the open bin is deliberate, to clear the cabling.

Beit Ha'Totchan, 2005: The rear interior bulkhead was quite busy. In addition to the switches, piping and cables, there were the air cleaners normally inside on the standard tank, an oil cleaner, four seats (three shown) and another rifle rack on the right.

Yad La'Shiryon, 1999: The rear-most floor plates are missing on this vehicle, revealing the forward portion of the Cummins engine. The missing hinged plates would rest on the two ledges shown. Note the subtle differences between this vehicle and the one at *Beit Ha'Totchan*.

Beit Ha'Totchan, 2005: There were 11 rounds stored on the left side, one more than on the right. There was also another socket mount for a machine gun on this side.

Beit Ha'Totchan, 2005: The radio rack was located at the left rear. The absence of a rifle rack allowed for the one additional round, on the left. The rifle rack, at the left, is the same one seen in the bottom photograph on page 39.

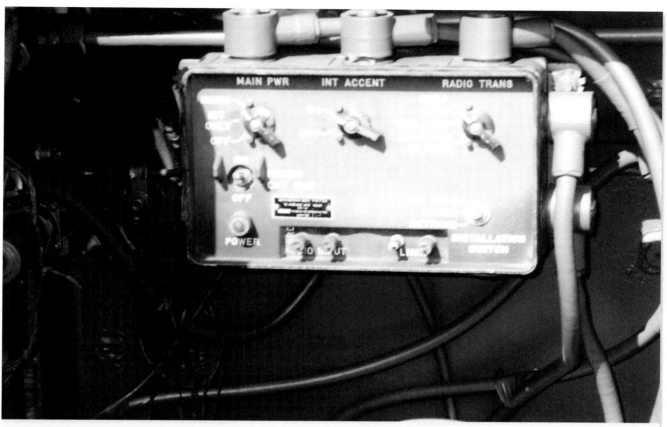

Yad La'Shiryon, 1999: Note the English instructions on the radio controls. There were separate dials for the intercom and for outside reception. Also note what appear to be connections for a field telephone audio, in/out.

Beit Ha'Totchan, 2005: This completes the all-around tour of the interior walls. There was one additional rifle rack, up front, for a total of seven. Note the same elevation mechanism as on the right side.

Beit Ha'Totchan n, 2005: This photograph shows the rear of the traverse mechanism, and the forward part of the driver compartment. When in action, the closed driver's windscreen was covered by a panel with tread-plate.

Beit Ha'Totchan n, 2005: The front plate had non-skid tread-plate, including the aforementioned driver's windscreen. The cover was secured by a clip when the plate is raised. The cut-out for the barrel rest was also covered by a flap. Note the different tread styles.

Beit Ha'Totchan, 2005: The driver's station was a standard Sherman setup with the exception of the instrument panel. This was repositioned on the transmission.

Beit Ha'Totchan, 2005: The former co-driver's station, covered here by hinged plates, was used for additional ammunition stowage.

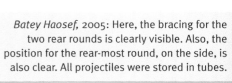

Batey Haosef, 2005: The large rear bins contained 15 rounds each. Six were stored in pairs, horizontally, in three racks. Another two were vertical, at the rear door, while seven were vertically stored, behind the side door. Note the bracing, just barely visible, beyond the horizontal racks.

Batey Haosef, 2005: Here, the bracing for the two rear rounds is clearly visible. Also, the position for the rear-most round, on the side, is also clear. All projectiles were stored in tubes.

These three photographs from 2005 showing the inside of the ammunition bin, are from *Beit Ha'Totchan*. Note the wiring for the tail light. The cable on the right is attached to a junction box on the outside, which then connects to the vehicle's field telephone and radio network. It also attaches to the telephone cable reel on top. (Joshua Weingarten)

Looking upwards towards the roof are the bolts for the lid hinge. (Joshua Weingarten)

Along the floor of the box are braces for the stored rounds inside the side doors. (Joshua Weingarten)

The following 18 photographs show a number of vehicles in a storage yard, awaiting the eventual cutter's torch. A number of interesting features are visible, including markings. The open storage bins, seen here, are directly below the side ammunition racks. (Michael Mass)

This is another *MACHMAT* 160mm from the same battery, in the same battalion, as the one in the previous photograph. That they are not the same vehicle is evidenced here by the visible mortar tube and different foul weather cover supports. Note the deactivated M688 Lance missile re-load carrier (left) and M752 launcher (right) in the background. There is also a launcher and missile displayed at *Beit Ha'Totchan*. (Michael Mass)

The front plate from this vehicle is sitting inside the hull. It is interesting that each time this vehicle was repainted, the ID number was replaced in a different location, at least three of them, in a very sloppy manner. Note the yellow air cleaner in the rear. (Michael Mass)

By comparison, the air cleaners on this one are the vehicle color. There is also no visible ID number, at all. It will, however, be present somewhere, as a welded item. Note the additional Lance vehicles to the right. (Michael Mass)

In the very late '90s, perhaps 1999, the South Lebanon Army (SLA) received 12 *MACHMAT* 160mm carriers. Based on published photographic evidence, at least one of these came from the same unit to which this one was once assigned. It appears that in the few intervening months before the collapse, the SLA vehicles operated in their original IDF colors and markings, including the '5' surrounded by the red triangles. (Michael Mass)

This is the rear of the vehicle in the previous photo. Note that the welded ID number is painted, for visibility, in favor of a separate, painted number. In contrast, the welded number plate on the front is in sand gray. (Michael Mass)

In this case, the number 810080 is not preceded by a *tsaldi* (the Hebrew letter symbol for the IDF). In Hebrew, letters are read from right to left, but numbers are read from left to right. The unit is the same as that in the previous photograph. (Michael Mass)

Here is still another variation. The *tsaldi* is painted outside the black rectangle, and there is no number within the black triangle in the unit marking. There are, however, two number 3s, one of which is under the marking. The front welded plate, in this case, was also once painted for visibility. Note the various shades of paint including what appears to be a yellow shade of sand. (Michael Mass)

Once again, this is the rear of the same vehicle. There are nearly identical markings here. Obviously, there is little uniformity within units. (Michael Mass)

Here is another interesting variation in markings. The painted ID number was not done with a uniform set of stencils. Also, the welded number on the left vehicle is on a plate, while the one on the right has the numbers welded directly onto the hull. (Michael Mass)

Here is another unit entirely. Published information shows that during the 1980s Lebanon campaigns, there were six *MACHMAT* 160mm self-propelled mortar battalions: 313, 322, 334 (which also included a battery of *TOMAT* M50 155mm howitzers), 345, 485 and 857. An *EGGED* was a group of artillery battalions, which may explain the unit marking, in this case, a white half-disk. There are several news photos from 2000 of a *MACHMAT* 160mm from this unit being driven by alleged Hezbollah militiamen. That may also be one of the SLA vehicles, since they were all reconditioned, possibly picked at random from this storage yard, and retaining the original IDF markings. (Michael Mass)

Here is a second *MACHMAT* 160mm from the same unit, as in the previous photograph. Its paint is in much worse condition, and there is a different number in the white half-disk. (Michael Mass)

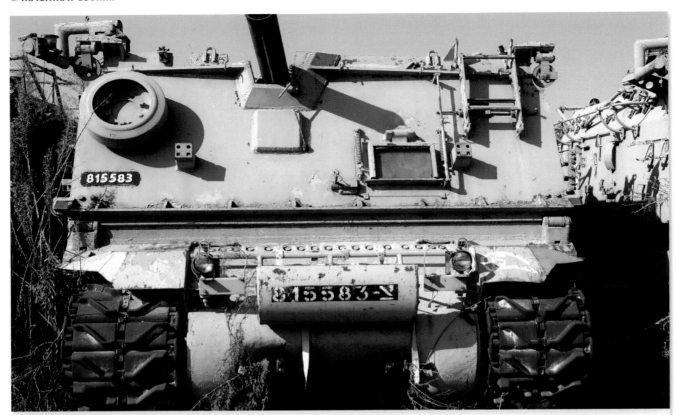

Here is yet another (third) unit marking. This just happens to be the same unit marking as seen on the L33 *Ro'em* at *Yad La'Shiryon*, before it was repainted. This lends credence to the idea that these markings were a specific *EGGED*, which would have included artillery battalions of different types. Here, the welded number plate is white on black, along with the normal painted number, which in this case is more uniform. (Michael Mass)

The ID number on this vehicle is unique in that it identifies its base vehicle as one of the earliest Shermans in IDF service. Several of these older vehicles were converted to other uses, such as a *TOMAT* M50 155mm, number 79044, subsequently captured during the *Yom Kippur* War and put on display in Egypt. One of the original production M-50 gun tanks carried a number, 79055, from the same series. (Michael Mass)

The number on this *MACHMAT* 160mm, 109188, is indicative of another somewhat unique vehicle. This one was converted from a captured Egyptian Sherman. Note that most of the vehicles in the yard do not have the muzzle brake. (Michael Mass)

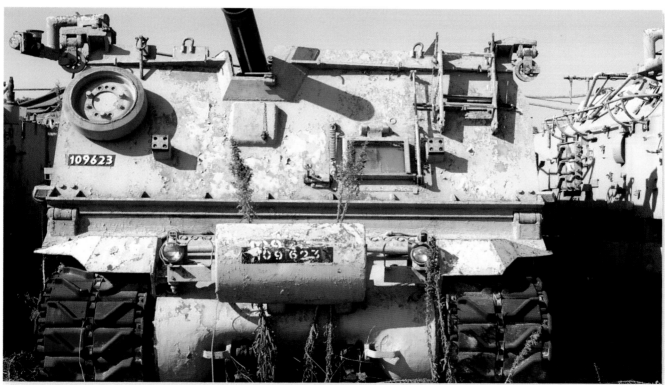

Here is another conversion from a captured tank, 109623. Such large numbers were acquired in this fashion in 1956 that it was quite logical to use them for conversions to specialized vehicles. Others were upgraded to M-50 tanks. Of course, it is entirely possible that one or more of these vehicles went through the M-50 conversion first, prior to becoming a *MACHMAT* 160mm later in the process. There are barely discernable unit makings on this vehicle. (Michael Mass)

Here is a third conversion on a captured tank, 109180. Other photographs from the yard show a fourth in the background. The number of that one is 109338. Back to this vehicle, it appears that the numbers were welded on, then painted for effect with a black rectangle around them. (Michael Mass)

Compare the chevron position on this vehicle with the one on the first vehicle in this series, from the storage yard. It serves to show different battery markings. Note the open door, in front of the ammunition bin. The left fuel filler cap was to the right of this, just inside the door. (Michael Mass)

South Lebanon, 2010: The SLA apparently did not re-paint or re-mark last-minute acquisitions like these, and ten years in storage have not been kind to the finish. The red paint was possibly applied by Lebanese Army retrieval crews. It bears no relation to either SLA or IDF markings. This conversion was done on an early short-hull Sherman, with a riveted lower hull. (Moustafa Assad)

South Lebanon, 2010: A second ex-SLA *MACHMAT* 160mm carrier sits among other derelict vehicles. The original IDF color scheme is very apparent in this view. Besides the overall sand gray, red was used to identify points of interest requiring maintenance. Note that the entire communications system has gone. The locking handle for the front plate is to the left. The driver's seat is in its elevated position. On a lighter note, among the detritus is an empty plastic water bottle. Lastly, the interior of the driver's position is painted white. (Moustafa Assad)

South Lebanon, 2010: An interesting detail are the various brackets and clamps along the side and across the back. In the background are some *Tirans*, also supplied by Israel. (Moustafa Assad)

In front of the *MACHMAT* 160mm carrier is another Israeli-supplied vehicle, an ex-IDF M32A1B3 ARV. The 'A1' designates the vehicle as having the horizontal volute spring suspension (HVSS). This particular feature may be due to an IDF upgrade, since there is at least one surviving M32B3 with the original (VVSS) suspension on display at *Yad La'Shiryon,* as well as an upgraded one, with HVSS and other signs of an IDF conversion, displayed at *Batey Haosef.* The 'B3' designates a conversion on the M4A3 hull, like the Yafo example. Unseen here, this ARV was equipped with the Cummins diesel engine and its associated engine deck. (Moustafa Assad)

South Lebanon: This vehicle was destroyed in an air attack shortly after the SLA collapse. This view of the right side clearly shows its origin as a short-hull Sherman. The insert, to lengthen the hull, is very obvious. (Moustafa Assad)

2 L33 *Ro'em*

Thunderous

58

The massive looking *Ro'em* was introduced in 1973. Here, one is on display for the press at an Artillery Corps exhibition on May 1. This is the *Degem Alef*, or Type A, as identified by the apparent extension of the upper hull. (Chanania Herman, Israeli Government Press Office)

DEGEM ALEF AND DEGEM BET

In 1973, Israel fielded an entirely new self-propelled howitzer, the L33 *Ro'em*. This was a rather cumbersome looking, yet very effective weapon system manufactured by Soltam Systems Ltd. It was an extensive conversion, with the original tank hull being stripped down to the tracks. As with the *TOMAT* M50 155mm and *MACHMAT* 160mm, the work was done using both M4A4 (Sherman V) and lengthened short-hull Sherman models. In this latter case, the cut was roughly beneath the gun mount, with the front weld for the insert bisecting the first large return roller, just as in the *MACHMAT* 160mm. Unlike the *MACHMAT* 160mm and *TOMAT* M50, the name *Ro'em* is not an acronym. It is simply the Hebrew word for 'thunderous'.

On top of the lengthened lower hull, Soltam built a large slab-sided casemate, in two different configurations. One style, *Degem Alef* (Type A), as on the two museum displays at Latrun and Zichron Ya'kov, featured an angled rear surface that was inset. This gave the appearance of a standard tank hull being extending beyond that rear plate. The other version, *Degem Bet* (Type B), had a flat rear plate at a steeper angle, with no inset. The effect was that the *Degem Bet* had more internal storage area. Depending on the angle of view, first appearances might even suggest that the *Degem Bet* was built on a standard short hull. This was because the appearance of an extended rear hull on the *Degem Alef* suggested that it alone was built on the M4A4 when, in fact, both types were built on long hulls. The lower rear door

59

Intended as a replacement for the M50, the M68 howitzer was developed by Soltam Systems Ltd. in 1968, with production starting in 1970. Its first combat use was during the *Yom Kippur* War, both in the towed and SP roles. Shown here, in the absence of a photo of the M68, the M71 was a further derivative of the M68. It shared the same carriage, breech and recoil system, but the barrel was longer at 39 calibers instead of 33. This difference is very clear in the photos, so the reader should simply imagine the area between the muzzle brake and the bore evacuator to be a little shorter. It also had a compressed-air-driven rammer to facilitate loading, at any elevation. Its range was out to 25,153 yards or 14.6 miles (23,500 meters). Completed M71 howitzers, along with some carriage parts, are seen here at the Soltam factory. (Israeli Government Press Office)

extension may also add to the illusion, but this is also present on both types.

The casemate provided enough room for eight crewmen to serve the gun easily. Crew access was through a double set of doors in the rear, single doors on each side and three hatches in the roof. There were also several other hatches along the top rear edge of the box, but these were not for the crew. The side doors were fitted with retractable ladders. It was 11 feet (30.4 meters) high and, fully loaded, weighed a considerable 41.5 tons. Later additions, to the *Degem Alef* only, included large tubular stowage baskets on the rear.

By comparison to the opening photograph, this is a *Degem Bet* with its steeper rear plate, and the simple appearance of a shorter hull. As described, however, both types have the same length lower hull with the difference in the upper casemate. From the front, both types are identical. (Defense Establishment Archives)

The Cummins engine was incorporated from the beginning. It was rear-mounted, with no need for a complicated linkage to connect the drive shaft, the transmission and final drive. Since the driver station was at the main floor level, rather than in its original place in a standard Sherman hull, a tunnel of sorts was installed below the floor to allow access to the transmission for maintenance and minor repairs.

The howitzer was a new design, although one derived from the French/NATO M50 howitzer. It was also from the Finnish firm Tampella, produced under license in Israel by Soltam Systems Ltd. In fact, all production, of the new howitzer was in Israel and then Soltam exported the weapon back to Finland. Designated the M68, it was meant at the time to be used in two other versions, besides the *Ro'em*. One version was a standard towed artillery piece. The other was designed for use in a fully rotating turret. The latter was to be compatible with any of the then current MBTs (**M**ain **B**attle **T**anks), but it has never entered service in that capacity. Both the towed and self-propelled versions had a muzzle brake and a fume extractor.

The standard M68's range was almost 15 miles (24 kilometers), although it was slightly shorter in the *Ro'em*. The barrel length restriction of 33 calibers vs.

39 calibers (for the towed version) was the basis for the 'L33', commonly used as its name outside of Israel. There are some published but unconfirmed reports on the Internet of a version designated the L39, with a corresponding barrel length of 39 calibers. The reports contain no photographic evidence, and there is no mention of it in popular Israeli sources, or from IDF veterans. With 60 rounds of on-board ammunition, the *Ro'em* could stay in combat for 20 hours, and it could fire all types of NATO 155mm ammunition.

The *Ro'em* was introduced into combat during the *Yom Kippur* War. Two battalions were assigned to the southern front, 341 Battalion as part of *Ugda* (division) 162, and 403 Battalion, in *Ugda* 252. The latter unit had previously been equipped with the *TOMAT* M50 during the War of Attrition. Some crossed the Canal into Egypt with Sharon and were, still later, transported to the Golan Heights. Eventually, they were driven to Cfar Hadr, below Mount Hermon, which is where they were at the final ceasefire. Three *Ro'em* units were still in active service during the 1982 Operation Peace for Galilee conflict, approaching and firing on Beirut. It was slowly withdrawn from general service during the 1990s. Although there were rumors that a South American country was interested in the *Ro'em*, they are being (have been) scrapped.

All new weapon systems and vehicles are presented at exhibitions, always for government and military officials and, sometimes, for the general public. Given the slight photographic angle, this *Degem Alef* is displayed along with its contents and crew at one of these exhibitions. Note that in this case, at least, the uniforms are one-piece overalls, with American-type webbing and American 'bone-dome' AFV (**A**rmored **F**ighting **V**ehicle) helmets. (Defense Establishment Archives)

The year 1973 not only saw the introduction of the *Ro'em* into Artillery Corps service, it was the last year for the traditional IDF Independence Day parade. This *Degem Bet* is shown in Jerusalem on that day. Note the spacing of the suspension bogies, which is visual evidence that the lack of the step on the rear plate does not indicate a short hull. (Israeli Government Press Office)

For some reason, photographs of the *Ro'em* in combat are rare. This photograph shows a pair of *Degem Bet*s in action in the Sinai, during the *Yom Kippur* War. The half-track in the background, may very well be the battery's fire-control team, in a *MAPIK*. (Defense Establishment Archives)

This *Ro'em* unit is moving out quickly, with the crews rushing to board their vehicles. Note what appears to be a Browning .30-caliber machine on the roof. Once again, this is a *Degem Bet*. (Defense Establishment Archives)

There was no IDF Independence Day parade after the 1973 event. However, there was still a post-*Yom Kippur* War victory parade in Jerusalem. This is a good view of the rear slope on the *Degem Bet*, unseen until here. (Israeli Government Press Office)

Here we see two vehicles in a depot or storage shed. While there are some differences in the markings locations, the two are essentially identical in terms of fittings. The gun aperture is open, with no apparent provision for a cover. (Defense Establishment Archives)

The ultimate fate for the *Ro'em* was the scrap yard and destruction. This one is almost completely cut down to the suspension. The photo does show the storage beneath the gun mount, more of which will be seen later. (Michael Mass)

There are two *Ro'em*s on public display today (2017). This *Degem Alef*, number 813237, was photographed at *Yad La'Shiryo*, in 2005. Its Sherman lineage is clearly limited to the lower hull and suspension, while the rest of the vehicle is new. There are limited markings on this vehicle.

This is the same vehicle photographed in 1998 in storage, behind the amphitheater before being put on display. It was still in its original paint and markings which is very useful. Note the different color of the M578 ARV (**A**rmored **R**ecovery **V**ehicle) in front of it.
(Doug Satillo, via Mark Hazzard)

Yad La'Shiryon, 2005: The underside shows how the casemate was attached to the FDA (**F**inal **D**rive **A**ssembly). Note the bracing.

As a comparison to the first photograph of a museum display, similar markings are seen here on another vehicle in a storage yard. Note that the side panel is fabricated from two pieces. The *Yad La'Shiryon* vehicle has a single plate, with no weld. (Michael Mass)

Yad La'Shiryon, 1998: Once again, *Ro'em* number 813237 is seen here before it was put on display. The large stowage racks were added to the rear sometime after the *Yom Kippur* War. Although the M578 is now on display with the main collection, the T55 *Samovar* to the left, as of May 2005, was still in storage. (Doug Satillo, via Mark Hazzard)

In this photograph, the lengthened hull is clearly seen, as indicated by the bogie spacing. In the original image, the welded insert used to stretch a short-hull tank is also visible, with the lighter line beneath the first large return roller being the forward weld seam. (Michael Mass)

2005: The second museum display is at *Beit Ha'Totchan*. In this close-up view of the left side, the two weld seams are just barely visible under the chipped paint. Note the line beneath the return roller, as well as the one that bisects the angled area behind the suspension unit.

Back at *Yad La'Shiryon* in 1998, this photograph shows the small hatches on the roof which would allow for ventilation on the move, without opening the larger rear doors. The lids double-fold to each side, one on top of the other. The two vertical bins are directly above the Cummins engine. (Doug Satillo, via Mark Hazzard)

Yad La'Shiryon, 1998: The original markings were still there, until just prior to the author's visit in 1999. At that time, the vehicle was still being re-painted. Similar unit markings appear on *MACHMAT* 160mm vehicles. (Doug Satillo, via Mark Hazzard)

L33 ROEM IN COLOR

Yad La'Shiryon, 2005: It appears as though number 813237 was converted from a hull that had not previously been fitted with the Cummins, as evidenced by the lack of a lower exhaust cover. It was, however, a stretched, short-tank hull. One indicator is the angled lower edge which is rounded on the M4A4 (Sherman V). There is also some indication on either side of the doors, barely visible in the original digital image, that the dual exhaust ports of an M4A3 (Sherman IV) may have been plugged. Although difficult to see, the lower rear plate itself is tilted, while the M4A4 had a vertical plate. This is a good view of how the lower door extension was attached.

The vehicle at *Beit Ha'Totchan*, in 2005, is also a short-hull conversion, plus it was once likely fitted with a Cummins as a gun tank. There is a very clear indication that a plate was removed, and the hole plugged. There is even an indication that the bolt-holes were also plugged. The method used on both of these vehicles is similar but, in this case, the obvious plug is on the left only. Note the circular weld bead to the left of the door.

On the other hand, number 815643, a *Degem Bet*, was definitely built from a tank already fitted with a Cummins. The plated-over exhaust port is visible to the left of the engine doors. Most of these vehicles had the new welded ID numbers applied in addition to, rather than in place of, the original painted number. (Michael Mass)

This is the front of 815643. These are in a storage yard, not accessible to the public. As mentioned, there is no front feature that distinguishes the two types. The baking sun has revealed the various shades of paint used over the years. The spare track holders are the standard style, seen on all sorts of IDF Sherman-related vehicles. (Michael Mass)

Number 813338 bears a similar unit marking as the *Yad La'Shiryon* vehicle, but this one has a '4' instead of a '3'. Unusually, the inside of the open door is darker than the exterior, even though the inside of the hatch was more normally the same color. Heat from the engine may have discolored it. The rest of the interior is painted white. (Michael Mass)

Several vehicles have evidence of white paint on the rear. The peeling sand gray reveals patterns that may indicate its use for visibility in the dark or the smoke of battle. This was evident on a number of *TOMAT* M50s as well, with the rear doors being painted white. (Michael Mass)

Unlike *Yad La'Shiryon*, the museum at *Beit Ha'Totchan* has its displays set among trees. This photograph was taken during Independence Day week in May 2005, hence the flags draped on or near most of the exhibits. This *Degem Alef* was converted from a short-hull Sherman, as indicated by the backward slope to the lower rear plate.

Beit Ha'Totchan: The M68 L33 howitzer was derived from the M50 155mm howitzer, which later evolved into the M71. The difference was the shorter length between the muzzle brake and the bore evacuator. The vehicle's interior was exposed to the front with an asymmetrical opening, and there does not appear to be any provision for a serviceable permanent dust cover. There are tie-downs for a weather tarp only. (Thomas Antonsen)

Beit Ha'Totchan: In this photograph taken from above and still outside on the left side, there is a clear view of the hand wheels and the gunner's sight which is tilted back. The interior floor is painted a similar shade of green as that used on the interior of the American M113 series and other vehicles. (Thomas Antonsen)

Beit Ha'Totchan: The same area is seen from the front. Throughout any action, the crew was almost fully exposed to anything such as sand, or worse, coming from the front. (Thomas Antonsen)

Beit Ha'Totchan: These photographs show both sides of the bracket used for a gunnery training device. The same fitting appeared on other types, as well, but only after the 1973 war. (Thomas Antonsen)

Beit Ha'Totchan: This overhead view of the right side of the gun also shows part of the right hatch and the rear of the travel lock. At the bottom of the photo, note the base for attaching the machine gun pintle. (Thomas Antonsen)

Beit Ha'Totchan, 2005: This view from the side clearly shows the size of the front opening. Note the overspray of white onto the exterior. *Beit Ha'Totchan* is located in a forested area in the northern town of Zichron Ya'akov, which itself is on a plateau overlooking the Mediterranean Sea. Did someone say that Israel is all desert?

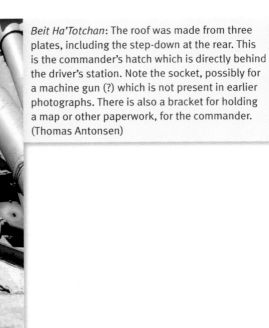

Beit Ha'Totchan: The roof was made from three plates, including the step-down at the rear. This is the commander's hatch which is directly behind the driver's station. Note the socket, possibly for a machine gun (?) which is not present in earlier photographs. There is also a bracket for holding a map or other paperwork, for the commander. (Thomas Antonsen)

Beit Ha'Totchan: This is the driver's hatch immediately in front of the commander, whose bullet-resistant window is to the left. Note the mounting for the driver's windshield wiper. (Thomas Antonsen)

Beit Ha'Totchan, 2005: The hatch, on the right, has the provision for a machine gun, but the socket is missing. The hatch itself is rotated to the left. On the day this photograph was taken, the town was celebrating Independence Day with a concert and fireworks in the town park, adjacent to the museum.

Beit Ha'Totchan, 2005: The open rear door shows the bracket for a field telephone cable reel. When the vehicle was given a preservative coat of paint, everything was hit including part of the interior and the exhaust. Note the mount for a spare wheel. The gentleman on top is the author's good friend, Joshua Weingarten.

Beit Ha'Totchan, 2005: Two large storage bins built into the rear superstructure, held tools, amongst other items. This one has the holder for the pickaxe head.

Beit Ha'Totchan, 2005: The next 24 photographs provide detailed information of the interior. Except where noted, the vehicle is the exhibit at *Beit Ha'Totchan*. The Cummins engine is located directly behind the seats. Ammunition is stored alongside, above and below the floor.

Beit Ha'Totchan, 2005: Here is the exposed engine. The radiator and its cooling fans are under the grill at the rear. Note the oil cleaner behind the seat. The latter appears to be long enough for four men. In service, a tread-plate hatch was in place over the engine.

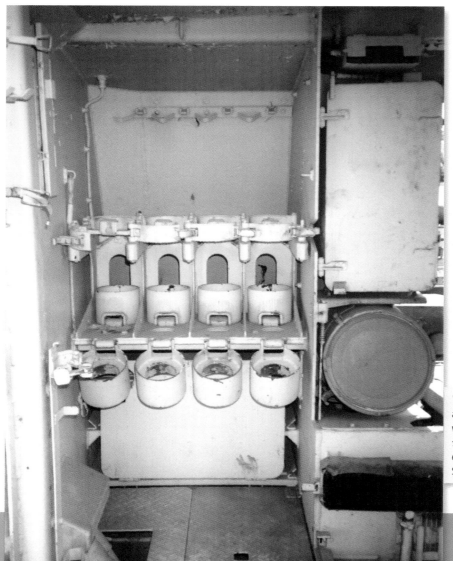

Yad La'Shiryon, 1998: Identical ammunition racks flank the engine. There were eight rounds on each side, along with 10 tubes containing powder bags. Note the closed door under the shell rack. (Doug Satillo, via Mark Hazzard)

Beit Ha'Totchan, 2005: The door helped to secure powder bags which were stored in tubes on the bottom racks.

Beit Ha'Totchan: The left side is a mirror image of the right. Note how the projectile racks fold down, out of the way, to allow access to the row behind.

Beit Ha'Totchan, 2005: The ceiling is relatively bare except for the bracing and a few cables.

Beit Ha'Totchan, 2005: On a gun tank, the vertical cylinders of the air cleaners would be at the rear of the fighting compartment, over the sponsons. The smaller sections would be inside the engine compartment, visible through the forward hatches on the deck.

Yad La'Shiryon, 1998: This is the inside of the vehicle before it was moved into the display area. It retains the engine cover plate with its tread pattern. (Doug Satillo, via Mark Hazzard)

Beit Ha'Totchan, 2005: This is the right-side door. Note the brackets for a fire extinguisher and two rifles, plus other fittings and electrical/intercom boxes.

Beit Ha'Totchan, 2005: The left-side door has one rifle rack, plus some cables just below it. The object, partially visible on the floor, is the missing engine cover.

Beit Ha'Totchan, 2005: Farther forward, on the left side, is the standard spring-loaded radio rack seen in, and on, many combat vehicles. Note that there is a noticeable lack of the standard stenciling seen in the interiors of armored vehicles.

Beit Ha'Totchan, 2005: The commander's hatch is above and just behind the driver. Note the folding seat, in its stowed position. Note the plethora of cables and other fittings.

Beit Ha'Totchan, 2005: The driver's station sits entirely above the sponson level. Designers added a crew access tunnel, of sorts, below the deck, which allowed for routine maintenance and repair work on the transmission and final drive. Note the commander's secondary seat to the left, and the provision for two rifles.

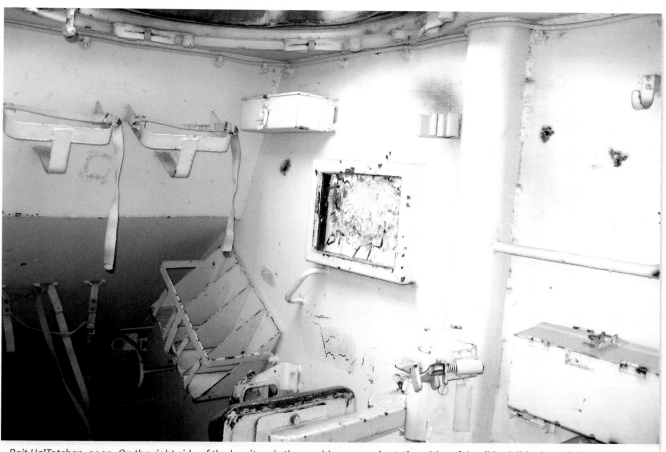

Beit Ha'Totchan, 2005: On the right side of the howitzer is the machine gunner's station. A lot of detail is visible through the open hatch. There is ample storage for machine gun ammunition, with two racks holding four boxes each. These two seats, plus the two, on the left side, along with space for four men on the rear bench, account for the full crew of eight.

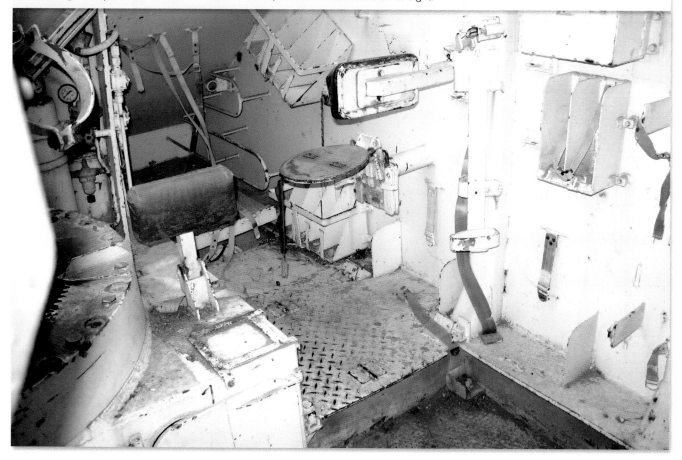

Yad La'Shiryon, 1998: The left side of the howitzer itself showing the hand-wheels for elevation and traverse.A literal translation of the Hebrew wording is: *"Warning! Do not grab onto sighting unit. Don't step/tread on the muzzle velocity meter"*. (Doug Satillo, via Mark Hazzard)

Yad La'Shiryon, 1998: The stamping on the breech block indicates a manufacturing date of 1976. Whether this also roughly indicated the manufacturing date for the *Ro'em* is purely conjectural. The same date is stamped into the breech of the *Ro'em* at *Beit Ha'Totchan*.

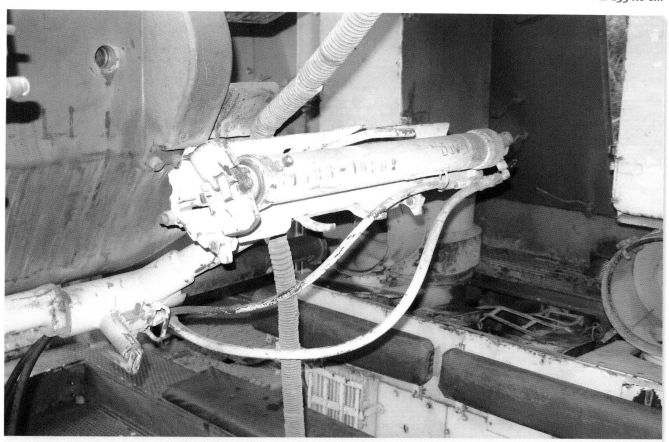

Yad La'Shiryon, 1998: Note the compressed-air rammer, similar to that seen on the *TOMAT* M50 155mm. The difference, in this case, is that the tray for the shell is fully attached to the gun, rather than a hand-held tray resting on it. From a different angle, in the photo below, the rammer is connected to a lead under the gun itself. This lead was connected to a junction box on the gear plate. The line continued from there toward the front of the mount. (Doug Satillo, via Mark Hazzard, me and Itamar Rotlevi)

Beit Ha'Totchan, 2005: The lead was then connected to the compressed-air tank which was stowed on the right side of the mount. Its gauges, and so forth, are stowed nearby. Those gauges are clearly seen here, installed safely in a niche, to the right of the mount. (Me, Joshua Weingarten)

Beit Ha'Totchan, 2005: Another similarity with the later model *TOMAT* M50 155mm is this storage tray for paperwork. Beneath the gun mount is additional storage for ammunition. Note the rifle rack on the side.

For a final comparison between the *Degem Alef* and *Degem Bet* this angle clearly shows the *Alef* (right) as having inadequate interior space. The shallower slope of the rear plate, and the fact that it is inset, are both indicative of this. Knowing that both were built on long hulls completes the picture. (Michael Mass)

Yad La'Shiryon, 1998: Large exterior stowage baskets were a common feature on many IDF vehicles. These were added to the *Degem Alef* after the *Yom Kippur* War. Note the jerrican rack on the inside face of the door. The second picture shows its mirror image, on the left, in this case on the *Ro'em* at Beit Ha'Totchan. (Doug Satillo, via Mark Hazzard and Joshua Weingarten)

This battery of *BM-24* launchers was from 270 Battalion. The action was near *Kibbutz* Elrom, on the *Ramat Ha'Golan* (Golan Heights) during the *Yom Kippur* War. Members of the 270 prepare their launchers for action.

Note the jacks used to stabilize the *ZIL-157* (6x6) trucks, a post-war derivative of the *ZIS/ZIL-151/152* series. A friend tells a story about the unit's radio call-sign in 1973. Chosen at random, the call-sign was *SHEKEM*, which means military canteen. A senior artillery commander claims to have been temporarily confused when he wondered why a canteen would want to speak with him. (Defense Establishment Archives)

BM-24 240MM ROCKET LAUNCHERS

Although multiple rocket-firing systems had been around for centuries, and mobile launchers were very successfully used by the Soviets in World War II, and somewhat less so by the US Army, the IDF did not become interested in the concept until the Six-Day War in 1967. In fact, until that time, all artillery was considered by many IDF officers to be of little importance. That changed quickly and the Israelis have never looked back.

The IDF used captured multiple rocket launchers of various types in small numbers in 1967 and 1973. Some of these were self-propelled, such as the Egyptian M51 130mm launcher mounted on Czech-built *Praga V3S* trucks. However, it was the Soviet-made truck-mounted *BM-24* 240mm rocket launchers, captured in 1967, which really provided the impetus for the IDF to study the concept. This launcher consisted of 12 tubular steel launch racks, mounted in two banks and welded together. Little progress was made

initially, partly over concerns about the availability of rockets. After considerable research and development, locally-produced rockets were finally available in 1969, bringing with them a corresponding renewal of interest for the IDF. These rockets were produced by Israel Armament Industries. Each consisted of a machined steel alloy warhead, an electric igniter and seven propellant blocks. They were fitted with an artillery fuse that could be set for impact, or on a delay.

To obtain the same saturation effect of a salvo from a *BM-24*, the IDF determined that it needed 12 conventional guns firing with pinpoint accuracy. Another less enthusiastic source claims the conventional tube artillery was equivalent to 40 guns. Either way, the comparison more than warranted their integration into the Artillery Corps. They were deemed to be such a success that they were extensively used on both fronts during the *Yom Kippur* War. As late as Operation Peace for Galilee, they were still in use with 9229 Battalion.

This *BM-24* was based on the Soviet-built *ZIL-151*. The difference from this angle is the use of a dual axle, which is a feature of this truck. The *ZIL-157* was fitted with large tires on single axles, in tandem. The photograph was taken in May 2005, at *Batey Haosef*.

Following the *Yom Kippur* War, the 270 was re-designated 9229 Battalion. The unit is shown loading rockets near Halbe, south of Beirut in 1982. At this point in time, the dress code was somewhat relaxed, apparently in deference to the heat. Note the number of fuse containers on the ground. (Yossi Roth, Israeli Government Press Office)

This 9229 Battalion crew may have acquired a mascot, of sorts. A little levity never hurts, particularly during a precious break in combat. Note the firing controls on the wing and the markings on the rocket. The location is the same as the previous photograph. (Yossi Roth, Israeli Government Press Office)

MAR240

In fact, the truck-mounted launchers captured in 1967 were so effective in 1973 that it was decided to develop even more powerful systems. The first such project was the MAR240 which attempted to mate an expanded launch rack of thirty-six 240mm rockets, with a turretless Sherman. However, it was not adopted for use in the IDF.

The MAR240 test vehicle is presently on display at Latrun. A careful look at the various weld marks and scars left as items were removed will often reveal a vehicle's history. In this case, the hull was originally an M4 (105) (Sherman IA), with its characteristic large travel lock. As such, it was likely re-fitted with the 75mm gun, as many of these early IDF Sherman tanks retained the original large howitzer travel lock. Subsequently, however, this large travel lock was removed, leaving the telltale scars still visible on the glacis plate. At some point, it was converted to an M-50, as evidenced by the visible scars left when the rear-mounted gun travel lock was removed.

The experimental MAR240 is seen here, during trials. The firepower of this system is triple that of a single *BM-24* truck-mounted launcher. However, it was not accepted for service.
(Itamar Rotlevi)

The rest of the photographs in this section provide enough information to build a model of the MAR240. Aside from the double rack for spare track links, the right side of the hull differs little from a standard M-50, one of which was used for this conversion.

From the rear, the weld seam at the sponson level confirms its conversion from a standard radial-driven Sherman to a Cummins. A number of other 'scars' means that other fittings were removed at some time. Visible on the right, for instance, is the hole where the original field telephone cable exited the hull. The mounting points for the box, and the weld scar for the M-50 travel lock hinge, are also visible in the original image. The tool arrangement on the sponson is standard for all of the rocket launcher vehicles.

The vehicle's origin as an M4 (105) (Sherman IA) is confirmed by the steep vertical angle of the upper rear plate. That of an M4A3 (Sherman IV) would be noticeably shallower. In its previous role, as an M-50 gun tank, it did not receive the final upgrade for the increased airflow, as seen on many other M-51s, M-50s and the conversions made from them.

The infra-red light was the same as those on the M113 series. To the right are the re-located siren and a side-mounted box for communication equipment. Note the vehicle alignment gun sight, as seen earlier on the *TOMAT* M50 155mm.

The platform was hinged to fold to the vehicle's left, providing standing room for the crew as they primed the rockets for firing. Note the bracket for a coil of barbed wire, a holdover from its days as a gun tank.

The rod under the communication box swings to the side to provide support for the platform. Note that the box is nearly twice the width of a standard box, as seen on gun tanks. Additional controls are housed in the cabinet on top of the hull.

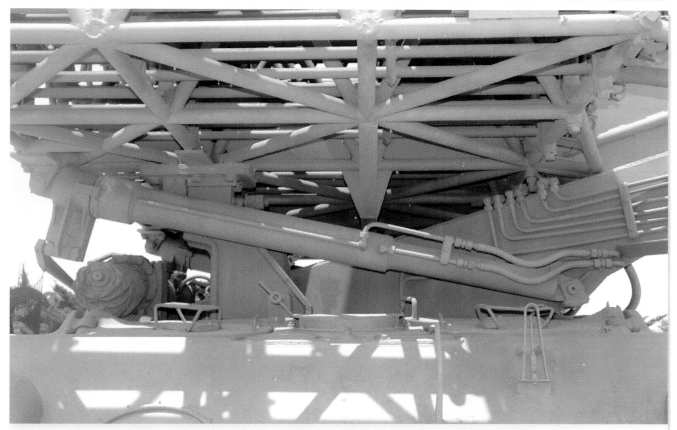

The following photographs constitute a walk-around of the launcher. Beginning at the front of the vehicle, which is also the side of the launcher, note the sight-vane for the driver. Most noticeably, this is not simply a matter of welding together the two-tier launchers, as they were removed from the trucks. (Josh Weingarten)

Note the dangling cables. In service, these would connect the launcher to the control box on the side. Most of this piping is electrical conduit, but several contain pressurized hydraulic fluid for the elevating arms. Note the re-located siren and the large control box. As mentioned, the rod beneath the box is the support for a crew platform.

This is a view from another angle. The electrical system is rather extensive, and multiple views are required to see enough of it to understand the layout. Each of these pipes carries the electrical cables needed to fire a segment of the launcher.

Here is a frontal view of the conduit and hydraulic piping. Note the small sheet-metal plate on the right, at the top edge of the glacis.

This view begins to tie the system together. The various electrical conduits begin to disperse from here.

This full side view gives an appreciation of the complexity of the massive launcher and its control system. The two large cables, one of which is braided and visible in the previous photograph, were connected to the elevating mechanism in the hull interior. Note that the original turret ring splash-guard was partially cut away.

The other cable differs, as it is segmented for flexibility. There is a conduit connection in the upper left of the photograph, which is part of the distribution network for the electrical firing triggers at each rocket location.

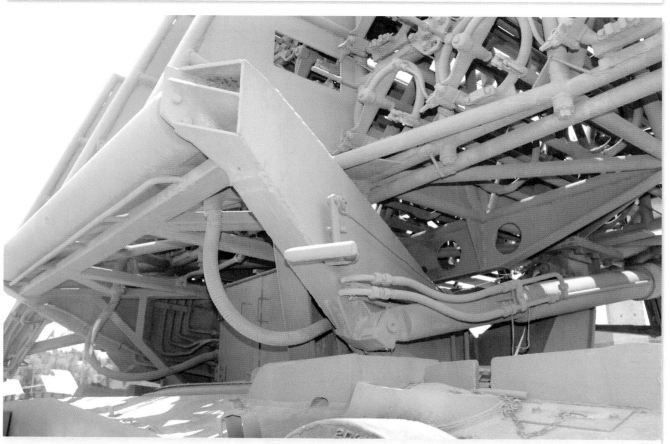

This completes the detailed look at the front and the left side, from the vehicle's perspective, of the launcher. Look carefully at the launch rack. The electrical conduit for the individual triggers is visible. The twin pipes on the elevating arm contain hydraulic fluid.

The engine deck was fully fabricated from flat plates, meaning it does not use any parts from a standard M4-style radial deck, especially since the base hull WAS an M4. Note the completely flat lids over the engine access openings, as well as the different style of hinge used on each. Unseen from this angle, the rest of the main deck plate was a single piece. Other Cummins versions used standard M4/M4A1 decks or decks originally fabricated for radial-driven gun tanks, which then had to be cut apart and the pieces re-positioned, sometimes with spacers. The choice of deck actually installed, sometimes, if not often, had no relationship to the original type of hull. This same style deck could be seen on a M-50 gun tank that at one time was in storage behind the Latrun amphitheater. That vehicle, based on a mid-production M4A2 (Sherman III) with the welded driver hoods, is now displayed at a memorial on the Golan Heights.

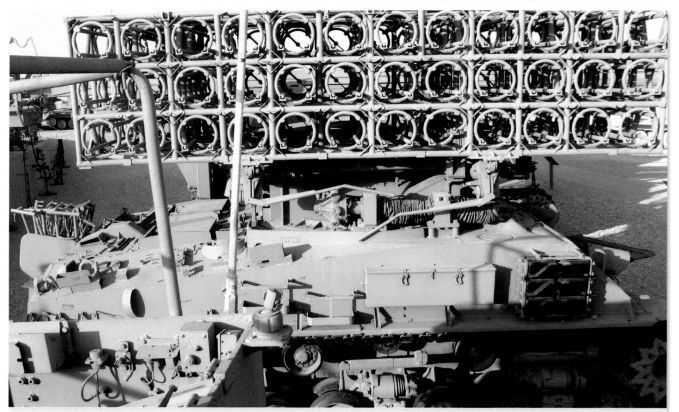

This right side overall view shows the general layout, as well as a lack of cut-outs on the turret ring splash guard, as opposed to the other side. An interesting feature of the rocket launcher Sherman hulls is the double rack of spare track links on one side, used to avoid giving up the extra links, because of other accessories. The foreground vehicle is a *TOMAT* M50 155mm, described in Volume 1.

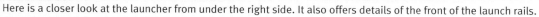

Here is a closer look at the launcher from under the right side. It also offers details of the front of the launch rails.

This shows an electrical connection and a sheet metal patch located between the spare track and the side stowage box. There are also weld scars visible, similar to those on the actual M-50 tank on display around the corner. These may indicate that this vehicle may date back to when the earliest IDF Sherman tanks carried grab handles in these locations.

These photographs, taken from the vehicle's front, show details from the side of the launcher from left to right, toward the left side of the hull. Note the co-driver's hatch in the foreground.

MAR290

The heaviest of the new rocket launchers was the MAR290 system, also designed for use on the Sherman. Developed by TAAS (an acronym for the more commonly known Israel Military Industries Ltd.) just prior to the *Yom Kippur* War, the initial rocket of choice was actually 280mm, given the name *Ivry*. It was tested on a single vehicle, a newly-acquired M548 derivative of the M113, known in the IDF as *Alpha*. Sometime afterward, a 4-rocket launcher for the *Ivry* was installed on a Sherman. This one-of-a kind test vehicle is presently on display at *Batey Haosef* in Tel Aviv-Yafo (Jaffa).

This hull may actually be one of the original batch of de-militarized M4 (105)s acquired in 1948. It is most certainly a former M4 howitzer hull, which at one time had its original large gun travel lock removed and replaced with a smaller one, suited for the 75mm Gun M3. The hull still has the mounting brackets for the hinges for the rear-mounted M-50 travel lock. A large, very complex looking tubular launcher, capable of holding four rockets, was mounted in place of the normal turret. After testing, the *Ivry* 280mm rocket was ultimately deemed to be unsatisfactory and it was replaced in service by a 290mm rocket. Even so, the MAR290 at *Beit Ha'Tochan* is labeled as '*Ivry*', albeit incorrectly.

There is also some confusion in some publications about both the name of the rocket and its launch vehicle. According to a source at TAAS, as well as Sagi Simon Tov, the 290mm rocket was called *Haviv*, while the 280mm was indeed, the *Ivry*. Both systems were mounted on the *Episcopi* launch vehicle. Once again, these hulls were converted from M-50 gun tanks by removing the standard gun turrets and interior ammunition stowage and then installing the launch racks on a newly-designed traversable turntable.

A single battalion, 418, entered service in 1982 equipped with eight *Episcopi* launchers in two batteries, for a total of 32 tubes. Launching a barrage of these weapons must have presented an awesome display. The rockets were fired one at a time, per vehicle, over a span of one minute. Re-loading was tedious, however, taking up to 45 minutes per vehicle using a specially-adapted truck. A special loading ramp was installed on an American-built M35 series 2½-ton truck, presumably making a total of eight such vehicles. The unit served in Lebanon during Operation Peace for Galilee, before being withdrawn from service in 1991, after being replaced by the American MLRS (**M**ultiple **L**aunch **R**ocket **S**ystem).

There are two *Episcopi* systems on display in Israel. The collection at *Yad La'Shiryon* includes one based on the M4A4 (Sherman V) hull. The Artillery Corps Museum, *Beit Ha'To*tchan (Gunner's House) in Zichron Ya'akov includes a re-load vehicle and an *Episcopi* based on the M4A3 (Sherman IV). Both hulls show evidence of their history as M-50s, although the paint on the M4A3 is so thick it is difficult to see.

There were only eight *Episcopi* launchers in service, all assigned to 418 Battalion, and two of them are on display today. This particular conversion was done on a short-hull vehicle, possibly an M4A2 (Sherman III) or M4A3 (Sherman IV). Both of these types had an extended upper rear plate and there does not appear to be a weld mark to indicate an extension of the shorter plate of the M4 (Sherman I). There is also a visible door extension. (Sagi Simon-Tov, via Itamar Rotlevi)

105

The same launcher is seen here during a test-fire sequence. The rockets were painted red, black and white for visibility during the demo. In service, these were an olive-green color. Note that the launch rack was situated in just the right position to avoid blast damage to the hull itself. (Sagi Simon-Tov, via Itamar Rotlevi)

106

The blast effect from a full battery must have been quite a sight. This is just from a single rocket. (Sagi Simon-Tov, via Itamar Rotlevi)

A crew from 418 Battalion is seen posing in Lebanon, in 1982. The hull was, once again, a standard-length Sherman based on the wheel spacing. Note the crewman standing on the fold-out platform, next to the firing mechanism. (Sagi Simon-Tov, via Itamar Rotlevi)

The same crew is seen here from a different angle. Note the air-recognition banner on top of the launcher, as well as the location of the radio antenna. (Sagi Simon-Tov, via Itamar Rotlevi)

Although lacking in detail, this photograph does give an idea of the after-effects from a salvo of rockets. The battery may have to move to avoid counter-battery fire or, theoretically, an air attack. (Sagi Simon-Tov, via Itamar Rotlevi)

In this case, however, launches continue beyond dusk. This photograph was taken from almost the exact angle as the previous one. (Sagi Simon-Tov, via Itamar Rotlevi)

Photos of the *Episcopi* in service are rare enough to say that this is the same battery as in the previous photographs. As it is undated, it is impossible to say if this peaceful scene is the day before, or after, the launch sequences previously shown. However, there is no crew activity and there is a civilian automobile passing by on the road in front of the battery. (*Beit Ha'Tochan* Collection)

The tarp does little to disguise the true nature of the *Episcopi*. Nevertheless, it does serve to protect the launch rails from dust and the weather. This vehicle was photographed travelling through an un-named Lebanese town. (*Beit Ha'Tochan* Collection)

The *Episcopi* with the 280mm *Ivry* rockets sits under the vehicle shed at *Batey Haosef*, in Tel Aviv-Jaffa. The hull was very definitely a former M-50 tank, based on a former M4 (105) (Sherman IA) howitzer tank. Also visible in the photograph are an *AML*-90 armored car mounting a 90mm gun, an IDF M10 and an ex-Jordanian Charioteer.

The tank's history is discernable, in part, by the scars left when fittings were removed. The lower set is where the tank's original 105mm travel lock was fitted. The higher set is where a smaller travel lock was fitted to accommodate the 75mm M3 with which these tanks were re-armed in IDF service. The square weld mark is for the locking clip, on the howitzer version.

The next 10 photographs provide details of the launcher and the *Ivry* rockets. This overall view shows the complex electrical connections and the rear of the launch rack. This was deployed in such a manner as to prevent the rocket exhaust from damaging the hull.

From the side the electrical system can be seen, and also details of the rails. Note the curve of the rail which provided spin to the rocket as it left the launcher.

This provides a detailed view of the underside of the launcher and one of the arms.

This overall view from the rear confirms the tank's history as a straight M-50 tank with its travel lock bases still intact. Note also the hydraulic arms for raising the launcher, as well as the rail upon which the rails rest when not in use.

Here are two images with underside views of the launch rails and the hydraulic arms. These also show that the launcher was built with tubular steel rails, supported by steel channels.

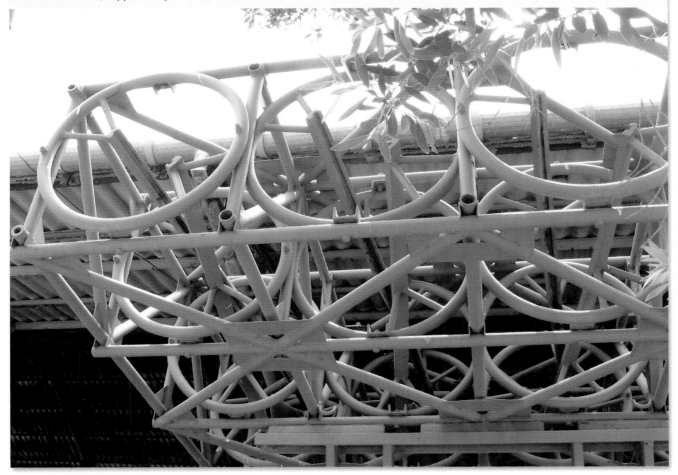

Here is a closer view of the flat rails used to spin the rocket for improved accuracy.

Following the *Yom Kippur* War, many Shermans with the Cummins diesel engine were upgraded to provide additional cooling air. The upper rear plates were removed and then re-angled outward from the top edge, requiring a triangular spacer. The effect was to give the welded-hull versions the general appearance of the M4A3 when viewed from a distance.

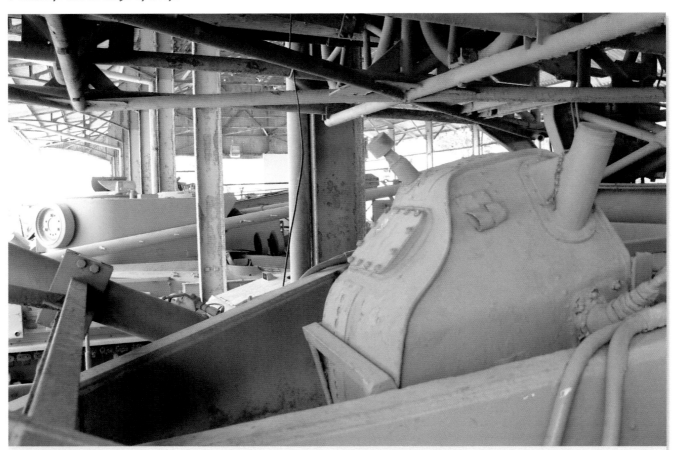

Part of the turret structure.

Except for the obvious fittings associated with the launcher and the Cummins air cleaners, this is a standard Sherman firewall, with the former turret ring still obvious.

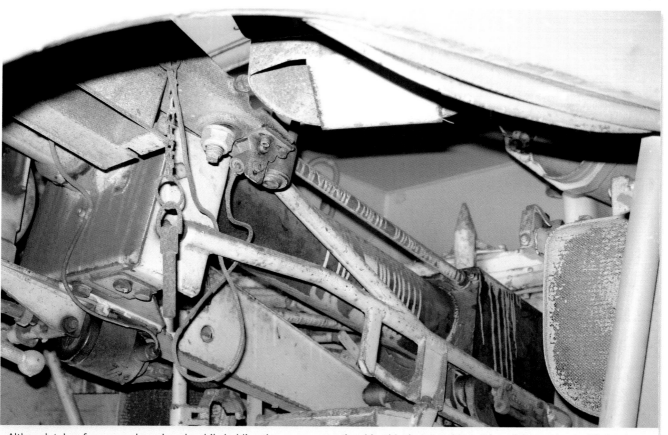

Although taken from an awkward angle while holding the camera over the side, this does provide an idea of the mechanical fittings within the turret ring. Compare this to the production vehicle, shown in considerable detail, below.

Once again, while not the sharpest photograph in this book, this is a further view of the interior.

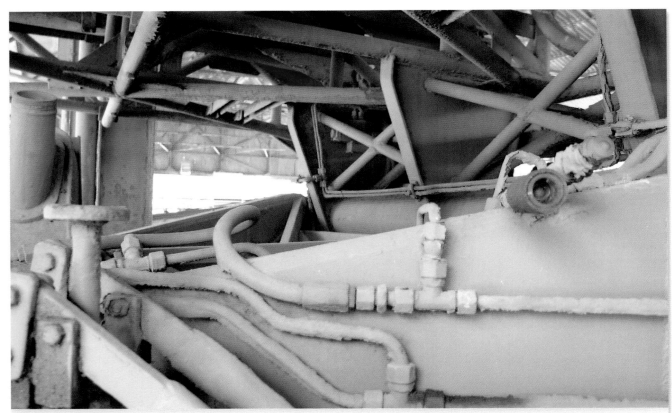

More of the turret and electrical system ...

This is one of several styles of air-intake lid seen on Cummins-equipped vehicles. This style is a fabrication done in France as part of its *transforme* project in which non-radial driven tanks were re-engined with the Continental R975 or, perhaps done in Israel. At the very least, this deck was installed from a stock of re-built types as the Cummins engines were installed. This hull would have already had a radial deck that was removed and re-configured to the Cummins type. However, it was likely placed in a common storage area from which decks were taken, at random, to be re-installed. It did not make its way back to its donor hull.

Note the almost triangular blocks added to the inside of the HVSS bogie assembly. These acted as supports for a bar inserted to further stabilize the vehicle during firing. They are installed on the front and rear units only, on each side.

Beit Ha'Totchan is home to a production *Episcopi* and its re-load truck. There are only minor differences in the launchers themselves. The obvious one is the 290mm *Haviv* rocket in place of the 280mm *Ivry*. All indications are that this conversion is on an M4A3 hull, and the outboard lift rings on the glacis identify this as a later production hull. Missing below the control box on the side is a folding platform for the launcher operator. From the front, another difference between the production *Episcopi* and the development vehicle at *Batey Haosef,* is the large standing platform on the glacis. The old siren has also been replaced by an infra-red headlamp.

The photographs in this section will provide detail views of the launcher and interior of this impressive-looking vehicle. One noticeable difference in this launcher is the lack of the round tubular braces at the end of each rail. Note that on the test vehicle, these are on alternating sides of the structure. Confirmation that the vehicle itself is an M4A3 is the lack of any modifications to the rear of the hull for first, the Cummins radiators and, secondly, for the added ventilation. In this case, the side stowage box is the shorter variety as seen on one of two versions of the M-51. Also, the support brace for the massive launch rack is different from the Batey Haosef exhibit. The screen hanging off the rear was normally fitted beneath the engine access hatches to keep out debris.

810791

This is, in fact, the same vehicle in its guise as an M-50 tank during the *Yom Kippur* War. The registration number, 810791, is clear on both configurations.

In these views, from the side and from beneath, the connections for cables leading to the control panel in the box on the hull side are visible. Note the pipes on the outside leading to the elevating arms, which are protected by tread-plate.

Note the piping leading to the elevating arms.

Piping leading to both sides.

There is a single pipe and a junction box on the other side.

The launch frame is secured for travel using a simple hook and release mechanism, one on each side. There are also two fire-extinguisher brackets on the outer portion of each vertical arm of the frame. In this 2004 image, the small screen is farther forward on the deck. (Eran Kaufman)

The next four photographs show details of the lower portion of the elevating system. The piping shown previously is for the upper portion of the extended lifting arms, viewed from the rear. (Eran Kaufman)

This is the center portion of the same area shown in the previous photograph, viewed from the front. (Josh Weingarten)

This is the right side of the same mechanism. Note the Hebrew letter on the filler cap to the right, which is inside the normal turret splash guard. It stands for *tav*, for '*ta'arovet*', which is a mixture of oil and gasoline commonly used for 2-stroke engines. (Joshua Weingarten)

From the top, showing the cable that extends over to the rear of the mechanism. (Joshua Weingarten)

The next series of photographs provides an all-around look at the vehicle interior, beginning with a reference side view of the turret and its hatch.

These two photos show the view of the left side of the interior. For one thing, there is a second crewman seat. On the rear sponson floor is the auxiliary engine to power the vehicle's systems when the main engine is shut down. To the rear, on the main floor, the two circular brackets are for fire extinguishers.

Looking down through the open turret hatch one can see the driver's seat, to the right in the photo, and one of the crew seats. The rack on the left sponson floor is for a row of batteries. Note the rifle rack beneath the seat.

Seating is cramped. Note the engine debris screen on the floor and the proximity of the jerryican rack to the seat. The large feature at the top left in the photo is the Cummins engine drive shaft coming in through the firewall. (Joshua Weingarten)

This is a view of the turret race mounting plates, top rear. Note the way the air cleaner pipe enters the engine bay. (Joshua Weingarten)

The crew access ladder straddles the chase for the drive shaft. (Joshua Weingarten)

The hull floor is partially covered to the right of the driveshaft. This partial floor covers the hydraulic fluid tanks and some of the machinery that operates the elevating mechanism. (Joshua Weingarten)

Right rear, with the second air cleaner and the standard Sherman oil cleaner. (Joshua Weingarten)

This is the right sponson, beginning with the rear portion of the hydraulic system. Farther forward, the cables and tubing leading from the hydraulic pump to the outside control box and the various parts of the hydraulic system are visible just behind the co-driver's seat. (Joshua Weingarten)

In this lower view of the right sponson, the connections between the tank and the pump are visible. Note the pressure gauge. (Joshua Weingarten)

A closer look below the flooring. (Joshua Weingarten)

These three photographs show the course of the interior piping traveling from the control center on the front right arm of the launcher, to the lifting mechanism behind the turret. (Joshua Weingarten)

This is a standard Sherman co-driver's seat, with a rack for the radio on the right and the mount for the co-driver's machine gun to the left, in front of the seat. The storage for .30 caliber machine gun ammunition is just behind the radio. (Joshua Weingarten)

There is additional stowage for boxes of .30 caliber ammunition on the floor, behind the co-driver. Unseen, next to the co-driver's right knee is a rack for a rifle. (Joshua Weingarten)

Stowage rack for spare periscopes over the transmission and part of the intercom radio system. (Joshua Weingarten)

There is a front set of turret race mounting plates and rollers over the transmission. Make note of the welds and the instrumentation. (Joshua Weingarten)

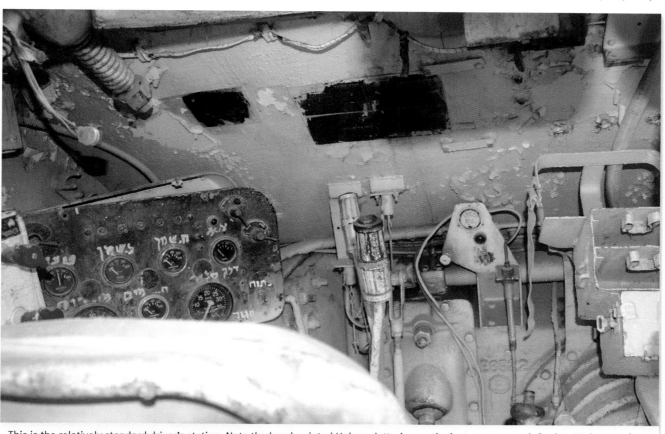

This is the relatively standard driver's station. Note the hand-painted Hebrew lettering on the instrument panel. (Joshua Weingarten)

The *Episcopi* displayed at Latrun is based on an M4A4. Note the suspension unit spacing. Unlike the vehicle at *Beit Ha'Totchan*, this one is fitted with the standard-size stowage boxes on both sides. Otherwise, the fittings are very similar.

Note also the rack for a cable reel on the rear that would connect the various vehicles in the battery. This vehicle also has the standard size boxes on both sides, unlike the M4A3-based hull

This is an excellent view, down the launch rails. The curvature that provides the spin is evident, as is the general layout of the rails and supporting structure. This area, within the collection at Latrun, contains a variety of converted vehicles as well as others that have added features, such as dozer blades and mine plows. (Guri Roth)

Compare the brackets for the launcher support frame with those on the M4A3-based version at *Beit Ha'Totchan*. Given the standard size launcher and frame, the brackets are angled upward to compensate for the different hull lengths. Note the raised deck hatch with its debris screen in place, and the extended exhaust with a tread plate installed on top. (Joshua Weingarten)

The casting numbers on the bottom of the M4/M4A1 style intake cover are an interesting detail. On the Cummins versions, the standard lid was simply cut into two pieces and then reversed. Note that the cut portion is to the outside, while the rounded portion of the casting is to the inside.

This view shows the hydraulic lines for the elevating arms, along with some additional details often overlooked by modelers. These include the small weld seams on the storage box and the jerrican holders. Also, note the bottom attachment points for the box. There are three for a standard box and two for the shorter version. (Joshua Weingarten)

This view of the left side of the turret shows the hydraulic lines leading from the hull interior and after they wrapped around the front.

These two photographs provide details of the turret.

This was intended to be a replacement vehicle until the introduction of the MLRS. The *Haviv* 290mm rockets were fitted in solid cylinders, on a modified *Sho't Kal* (upgraded Centurion) hull. The prototype is displayed at *Beit HaTotchan*.

EPISCOPI RE-LOAD TRUCK

The re-load truck is a converted American-built 2½ ton Cargo Truck M35 series vehicle, known in IDF service as the REO 2.5. The truck was originally designed and manufactured by the REO Motor Car Company. Later versions were built by Kaiser and AM General. This example is actually a long-wheelbase version designated M36. It is missing the debris screen in front of the radiator grill.

The truck would back up to the *Episcopi*, and the ramp would be raised and aligned with the empty launch rail. The crane, which is the same one used on the M113 Fitter, would lift a rocket from a supply vehicle and place it on the rail shown. The rammer would then push the rocket into the launcher.

673399

This is a close-up of the controls at the rear of the lorry. Note the alignment wheels used to guide the rails together. The lever on the right would then lock them in place. (Joshua Weingarten)

The controls from the front. (Joshua Weingarten)

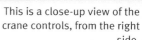

This is a close-up view of the crane controls, from the right side.

141

There are additional levers on the left. Below the crane is one of the two stabilizing jacks.

The crane from the rear. (Joshua Weingarten)

This view provides details of the truck and loading rail, as well as the crane controls. (Joshua Weingarten)

This is a rare photograph of the *Kilshon* in service, ready to launch. At its highest elevation, it does appear that some blast damage to the hull was inevitable. Given the bright colors on the Shrike missile itself, this is probably one of the original test launches. (Sagi Siman-Tov, via Itamar Rotlevi)

4 *Kilshon* (aka *Chachlilit*)

This Sherman-based rocket launcher was developed in response to the serious aircraft losses incurred in 1973 at the hands of Soviet-built radar-guided surface-to-air missiles (SAM). As with nearly all anti-aircraft weapons in service, this system was operated by the Israeli Air Force. The Shrike AGM-45 Shrike (**A**ir to **G**round **M**issile) was an anti-radar missile that was normally air-launched. However, the IAF decided to adapt it to the ground-launch role by mounting it, with a rocket booster, on the good old reliable Sherman, using available hulls like the out-of-service M-50 tanks. The weapon's turntable rotated through 360 degrees.

The ninth commander of the IAF, David Ivry (no relation to the aforementioned 280mm rocket) started the project in order to help counter the growing Syrian SAM (**S**urface to **A**ir **M**issile) capability. The resulting Shrike/Sherman combination was named *Kilshon* (Trident or Pitchfork), and it was first used successfully during Operation Mole Cricket 19, in June 1982. This was a planned campaign for Israeli fighters and fighter-bombers to eliminate the Syrian SAM threat in the Bekaa Valley in Lebanon, and also to engage the Syrian Air Force in air-to-air combat.

Basically, the Shrike targeted the SAM's radar dish when it was turned on to track IAF aircraft.

By deliberately flying an aircraft or unmanned drone into an area, thought to contain a mobile SAM launcher, the IAF hoped to force its crew to turn on the targeting radar. The Shrike would then be launched to destroy the radar, rendering the SAM useless. It contributed so significantly to the Mole Cricket 19 campaign that 17 of the 19 Syrian SAM batteries in the area were destroyed. Subsequently, 29 Syrian fighters were shot down without a single IAF loss during the biggest air battle since World War II. Its success rate was such that eventually, the mere threat of the *Kilshon* launching its Shrike was sufficient to suppress the enemy radar. At least two batteries were deployed, each with five launchers. Its role has since been taken over by more sophisticated electronic counter measures.

Two of the vehicles, as of 1999, were on display at the IAF Museum at Hatzerim Air Force Base, near the city of Be'er Sheva in the Negev Desert. The most accessible is based on a large-hatch M4A1 (Sherman II). The other, based on a composite-hull M4 (Sherman I Hybrid), is a gate guard behind a fence. However, during a friend's visit earlier, it was accessible to the visiting public, as seen in photos. Based on its serial number, 812616, this latter vehicle was converted from one of the M-50s photographed approaching Jerusalem in June 1967.

As mentioned, there are two *Kilshons* at the Israeli Air Force Museum. This *Kilshon* is based on a late-production large-hatch M4A1 (Sherman II). The actual AGM-45 Shrike missile extends back to the second set of fins. The rear portion is a booster rocket for extending the range of what was normally an air-launched weapon. Note the rather interesting travel lock. This appears to be mounted on hinges that include M-50 style travel lock bases. The display placard identifies the vehicle as '*Chachlilit*'.

This series of photographs, taken between 1998 and 2008, provides an all-around view of the two vehicles. Here is the front of the cast-hull version with a closer look at the M-50 hinges, adapted for the travel lock.

The launch rail includes a ladder on the side. Also note that at some point after the previous photograph was taken, the museum staff re-engaged the travel lock. (David 'Didi' Levy)

There are several notable features on this vehicle:
1. There is a double rack for the spare tracks, as on the other launch vehicles.
2. The frame on the transmission cover is possibly, even likely, the base for a platform to allow a crewman to manually attach the travel lock. Note the change of color between visits in 1999, to those in 2008. (David Levy)

Back to 1999, this photograph shows the attachment points for the hydraulic lifting arm, as well as the support arms.

This view shows the bottom of the lifting arm and the forward portion of the turntable or turret. Note the connections for the lift arm.

This overall frontal view of the launcher's left side shows the cabling for the launch controls, as well as the control position itself.

Another view of the control position, more to the side and rear. Note the gouges in the cast armor, caused by displaced sand in the mold. (Mark Hazzard)

From 2008, this is an excellent view of the rear of the controls. (David Levy)

From the rear, one can see the partial stowage bin common to rocket launcher-type Shermans, as well as the post-1973 numbers, welded directly to the hull and the seam where the late M4A1's hull was extended downward to accommodate the Cummins radiators. In the original image and in others, the weld scar for the missing M-50 travel lock hinge is visible. (David Levy)

The full right-side view shows not only the right side of the launcher itself, but also the revised tool stowage for the rocket launchers, the M-51-style double set of boxes, and an empty telephone box.

This hull received the latest upgrade to allow additional airflow to the radiators. The upper rear of the hull was cut and essentially, pivoted backward from the bottom, with a V-shaped insert added on each side. This increased the volume of air that could be drawn by the twin radiator fans. Note that weld bead was added to fill the gap created at the bottom where the fenders meet the hull.

The second *Kilshon* is based on a late production composite hull M4 (Sherman I Hybrid). In this case, the launcher is traversed to the left. Note also that the launcher is set at a higher elevation than the other one. (Mark Hazzard)

In this earlier photograph, with the vehicle in its original sand gray color, the launcher is traversed, but it is not elevated. Note that the rear plate is set at its original angle as built, although it was extended downward to allow for the Cummins installation. (Mark Hazzard)

Compare this photograph with the similar view of the M4A1-based vehicle. The M4 Composite shared the same hatch style, indicating a late production vehicle but, as built, it retained dry ammunition stowage thus requiring the appliqué armor. (Mark Hazzard)

Missing are the hinges for the travel lock, but part of the front platform frame is still present. The registration number of 812616 indicates one of a column of M-50 tanks, from the 10th '*Har'el*' Armored Division, shown approaching Jerusalem (below). (Mark Hazzard)

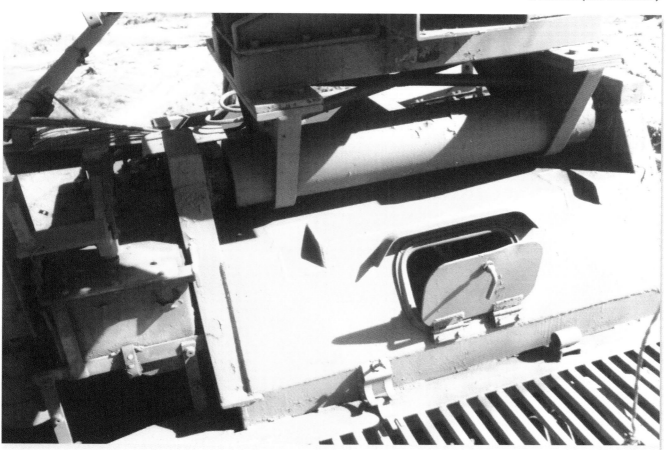

These images show the front and rear of the traversable turret which is bolted to the moveable portion of the turret race. Although not seen here, the interior portion of this will likely resemble that of the *Episcopi,* shown previously. The IAF Museum on the grounds of the Hatzerim Air Force Base includes a large number of aircraft. In the background are three transports, including a barely visible C47 on the left. Every historical aircraft type utilized by the IAF is displayed there, from early Spitfires and *Avia* 199s (Czech *Bf* 109s) to *Kfirs*. (Mark Hazzard)

154

This is both a contemporary of, and one of the successors to the *Kilshon*, named *Keres*. It is a triple launcher for the improved AGM-78 Standard ARM (**A**nti-**R**adiation **M**issile) mounted on a REO, an American-built M809 5-ton truck. The IDF unofficially referred to any American-built military truck as 'REO'. Introduced in 1982, it saw service during Operation Peace for Galilee. (Joshua Weingarten)

5 Eyal OP Sherman

Observing the enemy

One of these impressive vehicles is prominently displayed at *Yad La'Shiryon*. The sheer weight of the boom is evident in the size of the forward support arms welded to the hull.

This M-50 is shown here advancing in the Sinai Desert during the Six-Day War in 1967. In a relatively short time, following the war, it was converted to the OP vehicle at Latrun.

One of the more unusual IDF Sherman conversions was the *Eyal* Observation Post Tank. Israeli engineers had designed and built high sand dunes, as part of the Suez Canal defenses, known as the Bar-Lev Line. With the good intention of blocking Egyptian observation of IDF movements, the dunes also served to obscure any Israeli observation of Egyptian activity, particularly in areas where there were no fixed emplacements.

Soldiers have dealt with such problems for centuries, sometimes resulting in unique and innovative solutions. The idea was to get higher than your opponent, the proverbial 'high ground'. As an example, during the 19th Century American Civil War, hot-air balloons tethered to the ground were used. The dangers involved with balloons included wind, a large easily pierced target for enemy sharpshooters and a means for a quick, safe, descent in the event of a problem.

155

The concept for the *Eyal* OP Sherman is reminiscent of the hydraulic bucket lifts used by civilian utility crews to repair power lines. These 'cherry pickers', to use an American slang term for them, were subject to the same problems as the balloons, but the solutions were more easily managed, mechanically. Introduced and tested in combat conditions in the northern Canal area right at the end of the War of Attrition, the *Eyal* OP tank then served successfully, following the official ceasefire that ended that conflict. The surprise attack aspects of the initial stages of the *Yom Kippur* War meant that its usefulness for cross-Canal observation during the start of that conflict, was limited. One vehicle was even overrun and captured by Egyptian troops.

The system's design is both simple and elaborate, at the same time. A complex hydraulic mechanism lifted an observation platform 98.4 feet (nearly 30 meters) in the air. From that height, it was possible for the two observers, using high-powered binoculars, to see over the man-made sand dunes with a better view of the Egyptian positions than was possible from the ground. It was intended for use in prepared positions where the boom would be raised, and the observers would document potential targets on the Egyptian side. It could be, and was, driven along the road behind the Canal and used at short notice. Either way, the extended height subjected the baskets to the effects of the wind. To stabilize the platform when the boom was raised, the vehicle was equipped with hydraulic legs. Although this was not exactly a pleasant experience for the observers, none of the vehicles ever overturned.

Three conversions were done by *Eyal* Industries – the same company known for its heavy-duty cranes used by IDF vehicle maintenance crews, both on heavy trucks and on the M113 series. An interesting point is that these and other conversions were done using M-50 tanks.

2005: The legs were lowered first, to provide stability. The boom was then raised hydraulically until its weight was positioned over the rear of the tank hull.

This photograph was taken in 1992 when *Yad La'Shiryon* was new, and many of the exhibits were still in their original paint, at least at the time they went into storage. The massive size of the boom and its stabilizers are very evident. These vehicles were designed specifically for use along the Canal. They were driven along the artillery service road behind the forward positions, and emplaced when and where they were needed.

The logo for *Eyal* Industries is attached in a prominent place on all of its products, as shown here.

1992: These views down the right side and toward the rear, show some of the hydraulic piping going from the hull to the legs. Note the various layers of color, with several distinct shades of sand gray. The last layer is not as grayish as the one immediately beneath it.

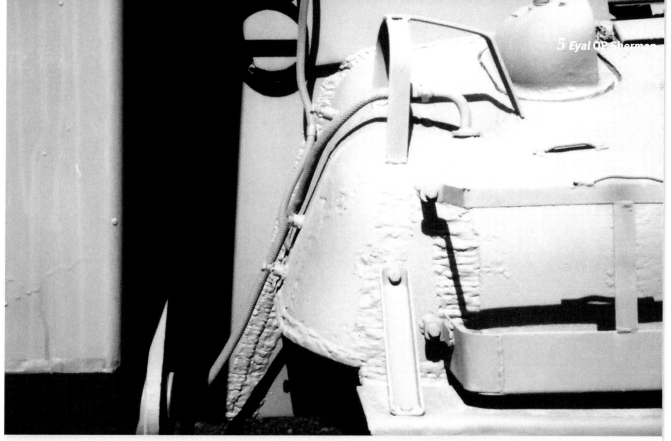

2007: The conversion was done on a mid-production, small-hatch M4A1 (Sherman II) that has received the modifications required to allow additional airflow to the Cummins' radiators. The rear portion of the upper hull casting was cut away and repositioned using an insert, tilting it backward and upward. The rearmost portion is no longer parallel to the ground, requiring additional weld material to fill the gap with the side fenders. Normally, this is considered to be a later post-1975 modification to Sherman models to allow for better air-flow to the Cummins. The longer M4A4 (Sherman V) and the M4A3 (Sherman IV) were previously designed to accommodate radiators.

1992: The standard Sherman taillights were moved to the rear of the leg module. Note also that there is a welded serial number above the painted version. As this welded-on plate was a post-1973 modification, these vehicles were in service for some period of time after the *Yom Kippur* War.

2005: Since this vehicle was converted from an M-50 tank, it was fitted with an otherwise standard Cummins engine deck with the louvres appropriate for the timeframe in which the conversion was done. It also has the later version of the exhaust mounted to exit from the top of the engine deck, rather than from the lower rear plate. Although popular opinion is that the relocation of the exhaust was done well after the *Yom Kippur* War around 1975, there is photo evidence that the modifications were actually started before the war. See my book, *Israeli Sherman, Second Edition*, for confirmation. Note the piping along the right side of the deck. Also, note the Hebrew letters next to the filler caps, which identify water (*mem*) on the left and oil (*shin*) on the right, and on the armored filler cap itself.

1999: The piping travels along the outside of the boom, toward the mid-level lifting mechanism, as well as up and into the mounting for the legs.

This photo of the left side shows the boom resting on the front frame. Note the piping underneath and along the side. The side piping leads to the observers' basket.

The next three photographs provide an all-around look at the basket. These three images were taken in 2005. The set of high-powered binoculars was mounted on the pedestal. (Joshua Weingarten)

There are also two seats for the crew, and a set of controls to operate the boom. Although it is not clearly shown, there had to be a radio/telephone capability as well. (Joshua Weingarten)

Taken in 1999, this photo shows the basket from the front. On the right in the photo is the second seat (partially blocked in the previous set of photographs), with a round bowl-like object placed there in the intervening years. On the left in the photograph is a small switch box, used for the radio or telephone, which would be mounted at the side of the basket. Note the piping for the control box.

2005: The driver's compartment is more or less standard, except for the piping for the main hydraulic lift which exits the hull through the bow machine port. Crew seats are in the middle. (Joshua Weingarten)

2005: Along the right side of the interior, fittings include the radio mount at the left, and the boom controls at the right. The cylindrical object is one of the standard Cummins air cleaners. (Joshua Weingarten)

2005: The vehicle's batteries are stowed along the left sponson with the other air cleaner. In between is the auxiliary gasoline motor used to run the vehicle's electrical systems when the main engine is shut down. Note the step to ease egress for the crew. (Joshua Weingarten)

Three of these unique conversions were built. For some time, it was believed that only one existed, as published or otherwise claimed by a few people. However, in the late 1990s, this second vehicle was stored in the Latrun 'bone yard' behind the amphitheater. Egyptian troops captured the third vehicle in 1973. Beyond the commonality of purpose, and the fact that all three were based on the M4A1 (Sherman II), there is very little standardization among the three. However, a published photograph of the third vehicle shows it to be nearly identical to this one, except for a three-piece FDA. (Mark Hazzard)

This photograph from 1999 shows the most obvious of the differences, with the huge base for the boom mounted at the rear. Unlike the vehicle on display out front, the entire lift mechanism is actually off the primary hull. This is also a perfect display of the fully-deployed support legs.

1999: The basket is enclosed, reminiscent of the type used by civilian utility maintenance crews. The front support frame is also a little different. This vehicle is distinctive in that it was also once photographed in its original M-50 tank configuration, just outside the Old City of Jerusalem in 1967.

1999: There are also treadways installed along both sides of the hull, which is not the case on the front display vehicle. Note the steps on the support frame, and the lack of piping along the sides of the boom.

1999: The left leg is not deployed, further differentiating the two vehicles. Note the massive size of the mechanism's base, as well as the control wheel. In front are an *AMX*-13 and a *Sho't Kal* (Upgraded Centurion), awaiting placement out front.

At some point, unknown at this time, the decision was made to return 811445 to storage rather than to put it on display. Here it is shown in storage along with many other vehicles, including a *Sho't Kal*. (Michael Mass)

1999: This photograph provides details of the front hull. Note the lone electrical cable going up the center strut of the framework.

1999: Due to the placement of the lift mechanism, the exhaust was diverted to the side and also extended. Otherwise, the vehicle has a standard Cummins engine deck.

1999: These two photographs show the placement of the right-side walkway. The screen actually belongs beneath the lid over the engine vent openings where they acted as debris shields.

The next three photographs show part of the interior from within, and from without. Note the levers for the hydraulics, and the switch box for the radio and/or field telephone that would be mounted in the forward part of the sponson. The white carrier is for a vehicle battery.

The details of the action in which the Egyptian Army captured the third vehicle are unknown. Obviously, even as other IDF vehicles were able to escape as their positions were overrun during the initial Egyptian attack, this one did not. Egyptian soldiers did take the time to pose for this image, source unknown, but presumed to be the Egyptian Army. Note that the base hull is also a small-hatch M4A1, likely a former M-50.

6 Medical Evacuation Tank

Ambutank

811881-א

172

This is the first type of Ambutank, otherwise known as a Medical Evacuation Tank. It is a one-of-a-kind design of two vehicles built. One of these is shown here at an exhibition for IDF senior officers. There is enough detail in the following all-around views to have a good look at this unique Sherman variant. (Defense Establishment Archives)

The War of Attrition (*Milhemet Ha'Hatashah*) was fought between 1969 and 1970, primarily against Egypt and Jordan. It consisted of mostly artillery duels along with an occasional commando raid, and some air attacks. In fact, some skirmishes began so soon after the Six-Day War that one may say that the 1967 campaign never actually ended, at least in spirit. During the fighting, casualty evacuation took place under fire resulting in even more dead and wounded. Consequently, the IDF Ordnance Corps was tasked with finding a solution.

In 1969, under the direction of the Armored Corps commander, Israel Tal, two prototype vehicles were built to test the concept of a Medical Evacuation Tank. They were both based on large-hatch M4A1 hulls with the conversion work being done at *S.D* (*Sadna Geiset*) 650, otherwise known as IDF Armored Corps Depot 650, located near Julis (a Druze village in northern Israel). This depot had done a number of prototypes, and also what the Ordnance Corps referred to as Echelon C vehicles, over the years. That there were two such vehicles converted helps to explain some visual differences that are discussed in the photo section. Then again, an Israeli publication regarding *Heil Ha'Himush* (IDF Ordnance Corps) mentions that a series of 10 such conversions on the M-1 *MAZKOM Tzar* (narrow tracks) was produced at *MASHA* (*MERKAZ SHIPUTS EZORI*, for Regional Renovation Center) 681 (formerly BMB 681). These vehicles served briefly during the War of Attrition, with each one being assigned to serve three or four *Ma'ozim* (Bar-Lev Line outposts, along the Canal).

With the concept approved proven in service, the next phase of the production process went in a different direction, based on the experiences of the design teams for the *TOMAT* M50 (see Volume 1). For one thing, it was decided to go with a longer hull and engine placement, to allow for some flexibility with the interior. In fact, the family resemblance is enough to lead to some claims that the Medical Evacuation Tank was actually converted from redundant *TOMATs*, which is not true. For one thing the SP howitzers were too valuable. However, the outward resemblance was sufficient for some troops to refer to it as 'M50 Evacuation Tank' or simply 'M50'. When initially delivered for service during the War of Attrition, these 'Ambutanks', as they were called by the Western press, were fitted with VVSS (**V**ertical **V**olute **S**pring **S**uspension) bogies and tracks. Over time, just as with its *TOMAT* cousins, they were upgraded with the Cummins diesel engine and HVSS (**H**orizontal **V**olute **S**pring **S**uspension). Development of the standard vehicle was completed by 1971. Still later, after the *Yom Kippur* War, they were again modified to resemble the display vehicle at Latrun.

Although these vehicles are generally seen along the Suez Canal in support of artillery units, they actually did see service elsewhere and with other unit types. As an example, Zee'v Greenberg, a former medic assigned to the 202 Battalion of the Paratroop Brigade, described how, in January 1974 after withdrawing from the Egyptian front, his regular unit replaced a reserve unit on the *Ramat Ha'Golan* (Golan Heights), near the Syrian village of Mazra'at Beit Jann, east of Mount Hermon. Interestingly enough, they traveled across the Sinai, through Central Israel and up to the Golan over three days, using cars and buses. Upon arrival, they found an abandoned Medical Evacuation Tank left behind by the reservists in bad mechanical condition. Even with a ceasefire in place, Syrians continued to shell the area, so they needed this vehicle. However, no one knew how to drive it! Since Zee'v had previously worked in a *kibbutz* driving Caterpillar tractors, he took on the task. The 2-cylinder gasoline engine that was used to start the Cummins diesel did not always work right, so he would remove a spark plug and prime the engine with straight gasoline. Improvisation is a hallmark of the IDF!

Here are two views of this concept vehicle, from the side and left front. Note that at this point it was fitted with the plain rubber block T51 tracks, including two sets of spares. The hull itself was once an M4A1(76), known in IDF service as an M-1, a number of which would be available from storage when this conversion was being considered, in 1969. The only 76mm-armed Shermans in service, at the time, were M-1 'Super Shermans', which had HVSS.

There is a very high percentage chance, however, that this display vehicle was converted from an early M-50, itself based on an M4A1(76). The potential tell-tale signs are the oblong plate on the FDA and a weld scar near the driver's hatch. The plate is the base for a bracket, meant to hold a coil of barbed wire, together with an L-shaped piece near the driver's hatch. These were not features of the M-1 series in IDF service. Note the weld scars where the original 76mm travel lock was removed. Another notable feature of this exhibit is that both sets of T74 tracks are on backwards!

To make the necessary room for stretchers and so forth, the engine was moved to the center of the hull, essentially replacing the fighting compartment. Then, the design called for an extended rear hull. The rear of existing hull was cut away, well forward of the idler wheel, in order to make the best use of available space before the rest of the extension was added. The welds are very noticeable. Note that the door's latching bar is very similar to that on the American-built halftracks, many of which saw service with the IDF.
Both views show how the roof is supported. The weld bead above the door tells us that this prototype/concept vehicle was converted by *S.D (Sadna Geiset)* 650, otherwise known as IDF Armored Corps Depot 650, located near Julis (a Druze village in northern Israel).

This overhead view clearly shows how the roof was constructed with prominent welds. Note the odd shape, as well as the lifting rings, and what may be a small vision block on the side. The blue vehicle to the Ambutank's right is a Soviet-built *BTR*-50, converted by the SLA into a similar-purpose vehicle, with an opening in the front. At this time, the museum staff had painted non-IDF vehicles in exaggerated versions of that user's paint colors, thus a rather light version of the SLA's blue.

The engine is right behind the drivers' compartment. The first photo shows part of a standard mid-production M4 engine deck, with the two filler caps inside the guard. (Joshua Weingarten and me)

The twin exhausts could mean that this vehicle still had the original Continental R975 radial engine. Note the smaller pipes exiting the ventilator opening on one side and the filler cap, on the other. The weld scars, where parts were removed, and the new welds, where parts were added, are very prominent. The filler caps have the Hebrew letter '*dalet*', which is the first letter in '*deleck*', or 'fuel'. (Joshua Weingarten and me)

These upper and lower interior views indicate that the designers and users made a very efficient use of the available space. There is room for two stretchers, plus the medical personnel assisting the wounded. Note the interior bolts for the suspension bogie units. (Joshua Weingarten)

This production version is shown here at one of the series of sixteen Canal emplacements known as '*Ma'ozim*' (see Volume 1). The timing would be late in the War of Attrition, or between it and the *Yom Kippur* War. Note the VVSS and the air cleaners, similar to those on the *TOMAT* M50, on the front of the superstructure. Besides the 81mm mortar, there is also a *MAGACH* (Patton) series MBT (<u>M</u>ain <u>B</u>attle <u>T</u>ank), providing additional firepower. (Defense Establishment Archives)

Referring once again to Volume 1, the Medical Evacuation Tanks went through the same series of upgrades as the *TOMAT* M50 series. This meant that they were rotated back to field depots where they first received HVSS, while retaining the Continental R975 engine, a process that was completed sometime in 1971. Note the radial engine deck, as well as the T80 track links on the glacis. To differentiate it from an unmodified earlier version, it would have its designation appended with *MAZKOM Rachav*. *MAZKOM* is the acronym for the suspension and tracks ('*Rachav*' means 'wide').

Granted, this is not the best quality photo, but it does serve to show the evolution of this vehicle. Taken during the War of Attrition, the picture shows a *Ma'oz* at the northern point of the Bar-Lev Line, across from Port Said. It was codenamed '*Atifa*' (changed later to '*Pelikan*' and still later to the more well-known '*Budapest*'), and was armed with a captured IS-3 Stalin, mirroring the southernmost outpost, codenamed '*Madved*'. The latter also had four towed M50 howitzers, while this one had captured 122mm guns, one of which is barely visible here. Note the odd-looking shapes beneath the air cleaners. They appear to substitute for the extended vents under the hull of the *TOMAT* M50. (Scanned from a book, written in Hebrew, and identified via www.fresh.co.il)

This is the version that was fully upgraded with the Cummins engine. This type saw service during the *Yom Kippur* War and possibly, a little earlier. Two of them and their crews are shown here at an undisclosed location near the Suez Canal. The stress and fatigue of recent combat are very evident. It should be noted that 'ambutank' is an invention of the western press. In service, the troops referred to it, as a 'Medical Evacuation Tank' or 'M50 Evacuation Tank', apparently due to its resemblance to the *TOMAT* M50. (Defense Establishment Archives)

It was very common for the IDF to use civilian transport, usually in an emergency. For instance, it was common to see lowboy-type semi-trailers being used as tank transporters, such as in this case. Often, these were delivered to a pre-arranged location by a civilian driver and turned over to the IDF. This Medical Evacuation Tank is being withdrawn from the Suez front in January 1974 as many reserve units were standing down and returning home. The writing on the side indicates that the trailer was owned by a company called 'The New Harbor'. Medical teams, consisting of a commander, driver and a medic, often served in a solitary vehicle assigned to a larger unit, in this case the historic 8th Armored Brigade of 1948 fame, near the Gidi Pass. (Photographed by a member of this medical evacuation team, via Itamar Rotlevi)

Apparently, a considerable amount of time was spent 'on standby', particularly just prior to the ceasefire. A supply of rations was kept on hand in case of a rapid deployment, or other circumstance that may preclude receiving supplies. The first photo shows a practical use for the side bins with the 'chef' who also has some personal photos taped to the vehicle, pointing out the contents of the 'pantry'. Included are cans of corn, chopped beef known as 'Loof', and grapefruit. There is enough for a single day's rations for five men, if needed. The second photo shows an alternative use for sand channels as sun-shelter supports. (Photographed by a member of this medical evacuation team, via Itamar Rotlevi)

The following series of photos provides detail information of this unique Sherman variant. The forward part of the hull is much more like the M50 SPH (Self-propelled Howitzer), especially the louvres, but there are also some major differences.

The sides of the Medical Evacuation Tank are quite different from the *TOMAT* M50, especially after the original side bins were removed from the 'Ambutank'. This left side view clearly shows where the hull sides are inset, requiring the use of standard fenders. Note the weld seams on the front of the superstructure. Lastly, it has been reported that the structure, at the rear, was an air conditioning unit. A veteran of service, in this type of vehicle, explained that it is simply storage, accessible from the inside.

This right-rear view shows two of the three rear doors. Two ventilators and a pair of smoke dischargers are fitted to each side.

All three doors are visible here in this photo from 1992. The brackets on the doors are for fire extinguishers. The registration number of 810150 is well within the series of numbers assigned to M-50 tanks, so it is highly likely that this vehicle was converted from an out-of-service tank. In 1992, the collection was still in the colors and markings consistent with when they were originally retired from service and put into storage.

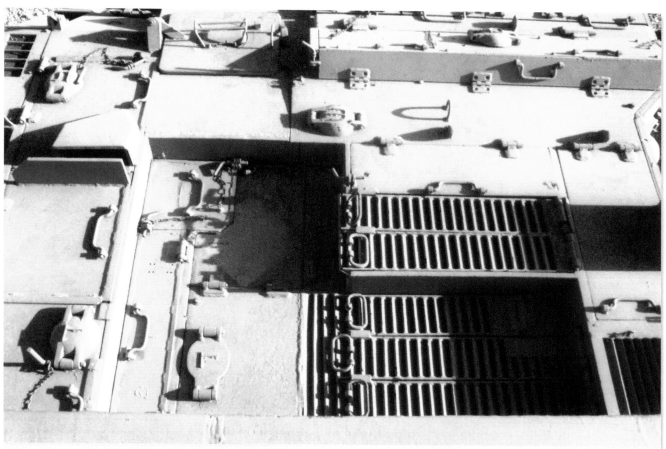

All-around views of the engine deck. This is similar, but not identical, to that of the *TOMAT* M50, further demonstrating that one was not converted from the other. The first photo is the left front, dedicated to the driver's station, lockers and fuel tanks. The second is the right side, behind the large set of engine ventilation louvres.

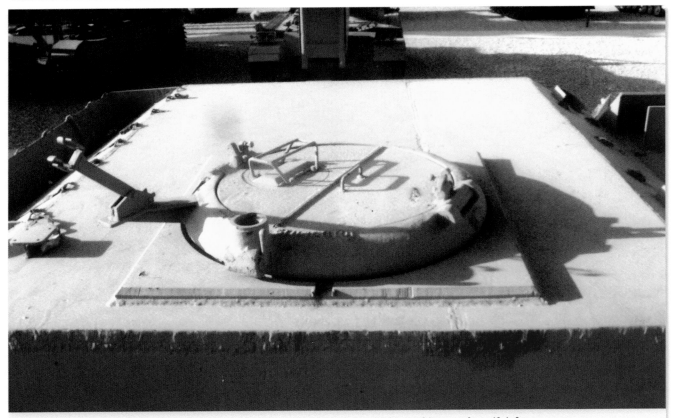

This third view of the engine deck shows the center and left rear portions. Note the rear of the engine decking, and how it is connected to the deck.

This view shows the commander's hatch. Note that even this ambulance carried a machine gun for self-defense.

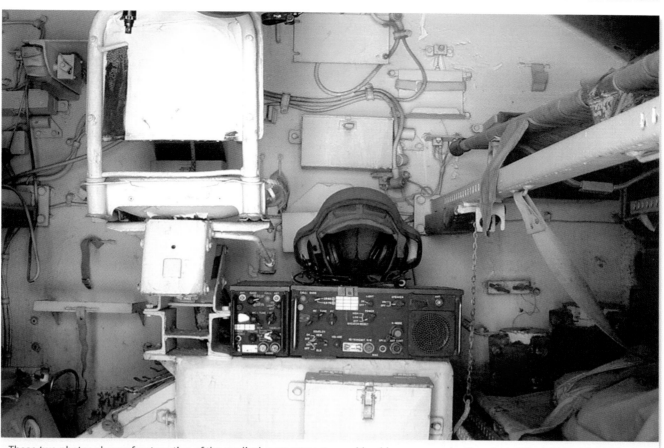

These two photos show a front portion of the medical compartment, considerably more complex than that of the initial trial vehicle. For one thing, the engine bay extends back into this area. Also, there is a seat for the commander, and a number of storage boxes, and so on. (Joshua Weingarten)

188

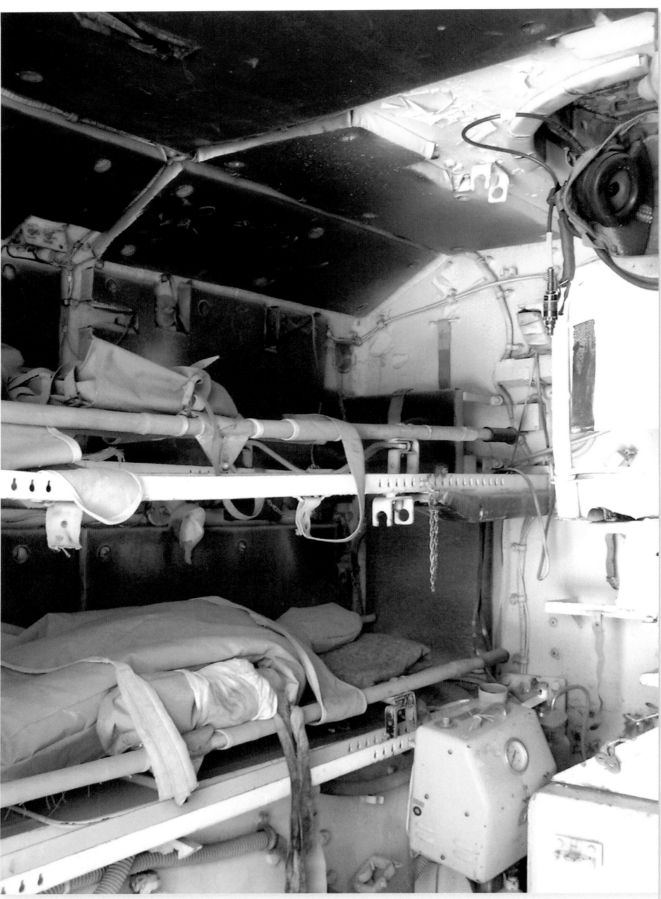

There is room for four stretchers, and there is even some cushioning in case of a roll-over or other severe movement, that may throw a wounded soldier or even the crew, against the walls. (Joshua Weingarten)

Lomed

This vehicle was often said to be a command tank, but more logically it is identified at the museum as a driver-training vehicle. It is also acknowledged that the modified vehicle was used by the Artillery Corps. This is a close-up view of the raised hinges on the glacis. They look very much like those on the *Kilshon* at Hatzerim. In fact, this vehicle has many features common to the missile launcher.

The Hebrew letter *lamedh* on the blue background stands for *lomed*, or learner. Compare this right-side view with a similar picture of the *Kilshon*. Except for the launcher itself, they are virtually identical. In this view, the round protrusion on the side of the hull corresponds with the hole in the *Kilshon*'s telephone box. Note the small bolt on the light guard that probably secured the light cover. Another interesting feature are the retrofitted fenders for the wider suspension. The IDF did not use sand shields, beyond those very early Sherman tanks that came with them already fitted, and even those were later removed. Thus there are no holes in the sides. When you see an M-51, for instance, with holes in the fenders, this means that it was upgraded from an M-1 Super Sherman which already had fenders, as originally built in the USA.

This is definitely not a standard cupola. It is, however, more than sufficient for a driving instructor. The cover over the turret opening is very basic. Most instructors in the IDF are female. (Jan-Willem de Boer)

The exhaust is the same style as used on the missile and rocket launcher vehicles. Note how it angles down to the bottom edge of the rear of the upper hull, out of the way of any activity with the launcher. At the top of the photo is a partial view of an M2 half-track, modified with the fuel tanks on the rear. On the subject vehicle, note the filler caps with Hebrew letters either on top, next to it, or both. From the bottom: The first cap has the letter 'dalet', which is the first letter in 'delek', or fuel, which would also appear on the other side. The middle letter is mem for water, and the top one is shin for oil. (Jan-Willem de Boer)

The left side stowage is also identical to the *Kilshon*. This is quite likely one of the missile vehicles, after the type was replaced, or when it was deemed that a sufficient number of active launchers were in place. (Jan-Willem de Boer)

The right-rear is also the same as the *Kilshon*. Note the revised tool stowage, typical for rocket launcher vehicles. Also note the welds where the upper hull was stretched. This involved cutting away the rear portion and inserting a spacer, of sorts, to provide for space for additional airflow, required for the radiators used with the Cummins diesel engine. Because the small-hatch M4A1s were shorter, the width of the spacer was greater than that seen on other hulls. Also clearly visible is the welding rod used to fill in the gap left when the rear section was tilted back and upward.

This view from the rear shows details of the various modifications done. First, at some unknown timeframe, the original indentation in the upper rear was filled in. This is the panel in which the welded registration number appears. Then, when the Cummins VT8-460 diesel was installed, the radiators required more vertical space, so an extension was added below, just as the lower rear plate was shortened, to accommodate them. The original lower rear plate doors were replaced with the extension and smaller doors seen here. Still later, to add additional space for increased airflow, the aforementioned tilt up and back was done. Look closely and you can see the weld bead used to fill in the gap with the side fender. (Jan-Willem de Boer)

At one point in time, stenciling was added to these jerricans. (Jan-Willem de Boer and the Author)

At the end of the British Mandate in April 1948, the last of the British Army contingent gradually left the *Yishuv*. This withdrawal took place over time with some units taking the troops out, but leaving behind heavy equipment for a later embarkation. This was the case with the armored regiment, from which *Haganah* was able to abscond with two Cromwell tanks which they used successfully during the War of Independence. Both of these tanks are displayed at the Latrun museum today. Here, an M10 unit's vehicles await loading onto a ship in the port of Haifa. Note that these Wolverines have the same type of overhead screens on the turret, as the vehicle in the next two photos.

Another IDF Sherman SP variant, with a lot of mystery regarding its service, is the American-built Tank Destroyer M10 series. Armament was always a sore subject among Allied tankers during World War Two, because the American 75mm gun M3 was soon outclassed by the thicker armor of later enemy tanks. It performed well against the *Panzerkampfwagens* III and IV, but the armor on the Panther, from the front, and the Tiger, all over, was just too thick. The problem was only made worse by the fact that US Army doctrine stressed that tanks were not meant

to fight other tanks. That task was left to so-called 'tank destroyers'. However, US tank destroyers had open turret tops, and even thinner armor than the tanks. In the Army's opinion, the 75mm gun was more than adequate for the tank's intended purpose of supporting infantry and exploiting breakthroughs. It was only after the war that this doctrine completely changed, at least with the American armed forces.

In 1955, Israel was in an entirely difficult set of circumstances in that they were in desperate need of weapons, especially since its Arab adversaries were receiving aid from the Soviet Union. Concurrent with the acquisition of French Sherman tanks armed with the standard World War 2 weapons, as built, there were also discussions about whether to purchase from France its new tank, the *AMX*-13. Officially designated *Char* 13-75 *Modèle* 51, this was a light tank, more like a tank destroyer – lightly armored and fast with a more powerful gun relative to its armor. In an interesting twist, this long-barreled 75mm gun mounted in an innovative oscillating turret with an auto-loader, was adapted from the *KwK* 42(L/70) 75mm cannon from the World War 2 German Panther. Since the French Army used a small number of Panthers in post-war service, it made an additional impression regarding the value of the gun, even after having experienced its power as an adversary. Being very impressed with the gun's performance, while also faced with a limited budget that restricted the number of *AMX*-13s purchased, the IDF decided to adapt the gun for use in available Sherman variants.

Just as an M4A2 (Sherman III) was used for tests involving the Sherman series, another experimental vehicle was an M10. As designed, the M10 was an open-topped and lightly-armored tank destroyer with a more powerful gun, a variant of the U.S. Navy 3-inch cannon. Therefore, the IDF intended to carry that same concept forward using the *AMX*-13 cannon that was re-designated as the *CN* 75-50. The fact that the only M10 variants on display in Israel looked very much like the British 17-pounder-armed Achilles tank destroyer confuses things by giving the impression that they arrived in-country, as such. In reality, M10s arrived in Israel in two ways. One of them was the aforementioned test vehicle, while the rest were among 20 derelict American M10 series TDs, specifically acquired for conversion with the French gun.

Subsequently, the M10 conversions were a disappointment, and British 17-pounders were installed creating a vehicle identical in concept to the Achilles. Regardless of the gun, the M10s were used for a very brief period as recon vehicles, not battle 'tanks', as originally hoped. This latter point was confirmed in 2005 when my friend, Josh Weingarten and I, had the good fortune of meeting an IDF M10 veteran in a Jerusalem restaurant. A number of these double conversions still exist, with two on display at *Yad La'Shiryon*, near Latrun, and at *Batey Haosef*, in Tel Aviv-Jaffa.

Here is another M10, again with the 3-inch gun but this time it belongs to a Danish regiment. Denmark maintained a number of units under British command during World War II, and this one stayed on in Palestine afterward.

This photo is often erroneously described as showing an Israeli M10 when, in fact, it is a British Wolverine with the standard 3-inch gun. The location is a *kibbutz* or *moshav* with some of the local residents posing with British troops. There were a number of British armored units in the *Yishuv* during the Mandate period.

195

As mentioned, the French co-operated with IDF technicians and engineers in the design of two Sherman variants intended to mount the *CN* 75-50 derivative of the former German Panther cannon, mounted in the *AMX*-13. The M-50 prototype, an M4A2 (Sherman III) named 'Corse' is covered elsewhere in another book(s). This is the M10 version which the IDF also meant to carry the same gun. Note that this is an early type which still has the large bolts on the sides of the turret and hull, plus the short turret counterweight. At this point in time, it retained its French registration number on the FDA.

196

This may be the same vehicle in an IDF depot. It has the same short counterweight as in the previous photo. At this time, the turret has an IDF registration number which may mean that it is one of the other vehicles armed with the *CN 75-50*. (Defense Establishment Archives)

At first glance, given the presence of the large bolts, one may be tempted to say that this is the prototype. However, this vehicle has a later version of counterweight on the turret, so it is one of the 20 M10s purchased for the program. The four men in the olive drab uniforms look like IDF soldiers, while the man on the glacis could even be a French technician, sent to assist the Israelis. (Defense Establishment Archives)

This is definitely one of that batch of 20 M10s, because it is a very late production version. Note the lack of bolts everywhere, except on the glacis. A careful look at the original digital image confirms that the muzzle brake is the type used on the *CN* 75-50. It is also possible that this vehicle has a camouflage scheme, but the darker patches may simply be stains or dirt. (Defense Establishment Archives)

This is a totally different M10, clearly marked with Hebrew letters and without stains or camo paint. It is another later production vehicle, more likely to be used late in the war in the Philippines, the source location for the 20 tank destroyers purchased for conversion. These TDs were fitted with the *CN* 75-50 for a short period, but the results were unsatisfactory to the IDF. Subsequently, they were fitted with the British 17-pounder resulting in what many erroneously refer to as Achilles IICs, two of which are on display in Israel today. Even these re-armed vehicles did not fit well in IDF service, and they were withdrawn rather quickly. During our 2005 trip to Israel, Joshua Weingarten and I had a brief casual conversation with a former M10 crewman, and he confirmed that they performed in a recon role only. Unseen here, these same people were photographed at this same location with newly-arrived *AMX*-13 tanks. (Defense Establishment Archives)

The exact dates for these photos are unknown. However, these M10s have clearly been fitted with the 17-pounder, and fully upgraded with many new fittings not present on the previously shown vehicles. They have the same style of smoke dischargers seen on the IDF Sherman tank variants, although the second vehicle has only the brackets. There are also spare track holders, jerrican holders, rear deck stowage boxes, Sherman-style external gun sights, spotlights and new radio antenna locations. Note that the indentation for the old antenna, on the forward right side of the hull, is now plated over and that they are both late model vehicles. (Defense Establishment Archives)

This photo is also undated. While there are indications that this may be a display vehicle, there is a cover over what may be a machine gun mount, unusual for such a display. It still has its registration number. (source unknown, via the Internet)

The IDF referred to the re-gunned M10 (which is technically not an 'Achilles') as a 'Tzalaf'. Specifically, in Hebrew, this is the name for a caper bush. However, according to Michael Mass (curator at Latrun), here it is used to mean 'sniper' which makes sense given the long-range accuracy of the QF 17-pounder gun. As can be seen here the ultimate destination for these vehicles was this storage yard. The faint blue Hebrew lettering on the side is Michael's mark, reserving for possible use at the Latrun museum. (Michael Mass)

This turretless M10 was possibly converted to a tug of some sort. My basis for that assumption is the Hebrew wording that reads 'I feel good in the Transportation Corps'. Note the bolts on the hull indicating an early or intermediate production vehicle. Also, note the darker oval near the front which is the plated over original antenna location. The front of the vehicle has fittings appropriate for a tug, including a towing hitch and tubular posts that may be the bases for some sort of tow bar or derrick. (Michael Mass)

A close-up of the left front corner of the turetless M10 from the previous page.

This M10 is in the same storage yard, and is also marked by Michael Mass as a reserve for the Latrun collection. However, the condition of the welds along the rear of the hull, plus the bent hand rail on the turret, do not match the display there, nor the one in Jaffa. Beyond the *Tzalaf* is a *Sho't Kal* and the *Eyal* Observation Post tank that was behind the Latrun amphitheater. (Michael Mass)

This is the *Tzalaf* on display at *Yad La'Shiryon*, near the town of Latrun. It has many of the same features as the M-50, including the same type of lifting ring on the turret side. Since this was a standard feature of the as-built M10, this is the likely source for that feature on the tank turret. Also, the glacis and the FDA have the brackets for the barbed wire coil and tow cable. Given the small protrusions on the center-line of the tracklinks, these are T54E1 tracks. The exhaust pipes are standard for the basic M10 which was equipped with the twin General Motors diesels of the M4A2. The M10A1 was powered by the Ford engine that was standard on the M4A3.

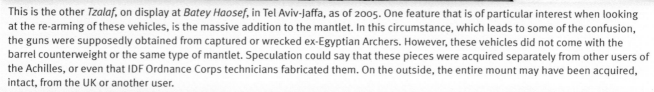

This is the other *Tzalaf*, on display at *Batey Haosef*, in Tel Aviv-Jaffa, as of 2005. One feature that is of particular interest when looking at the re-arming of these vehicles, is the massive addition to the mantlet. In this circumstance, which leads to some of the confusion, the guns were supposedly obtained from captured or wrecked ex-Egyptian Archers. However, these vehicles did not come with the barrel counterweight or the same type of mantlet. Speculation could say that these pieces were acquired separately from other users of the Achilles, or even that IDF Ordnance Corps technicians fabricated them. On the outside, the entire mount may have been acquired, intact, from the UK or another user.

The folding rods are an original American feature intended to hold a foul-weather tarpaulin. The spotlight mount is an IDF addition, as are the blade sight and the mount over the mantlet intended for the larger spotlight seen on other Israeli tanks. Note the details on the smoke discharger mounts. Lastly, the strips for attaching a canvas cover for the mantlet are also an Israeli addition.

The three following photos provide a general walk-around view of the turret interior. The communication equipment was mounted on the lower of the two flat shelves, with the top one providing some protection. Two of the images show the socket for the rear-mounted .50-caliber Browning M2HB (**H**eavy **B**arrel). There is a lot of detail in these three photos.

These last three images (continued on page 206) show details of the engine bay which will also be typical for any GM diesel-powered tank. Note the sheet of metal hanging in the center, removing any possibility of seeing the engine through the louvres. These photos were taken at Latrun.

APPENDICES

Term	Definition
...im	plural in Hebrew
Alef	Hebrew letter A
Batey Haosef	IDF Collection Houses, in Tel Aviv-Yafo (Jaffa)
Beit Ha'Totchan	Hewbrew for 'Gunners' House' or 'House of Artillerymen', in Zichron Ya'Akov
Bet	Hebrew letter B
Dalet	Hebrew letter D
Degem	Type
EGGED	Collection of artillery battalions, equivalent to a brigade
Egged	Israel Transport Cooperative Society, Ltd = Israel's largest bus company
Episcopi	Hebrew name for Sherman-based rocket launcher
Gimel	Hebrew letter C
Haviv	290mm rockets, mounted on the Episcopi
Heil Ha'Shiryon	IDF Armoured Corps
Heil Ha'Totchanim	IDF Artillery Corps
HVSS	Horizontal Volute Spring Suspension (wide tracks)
Ivry	280mm rockets mounted on prototype for Episcopi
kibbutz	agricultural settlement
Kilshon	Hebrew name for Sherman-based anti-radar rocket launcher
L33	length of howitzer barrel in Ro'em, often used in place of the name
La'Shiryon	Armored Corps Memorial and Museum, in Latrun
ma'oz	'castle keep', used to describe forts along the Bar-Lev Line
MACHMAT	Hebrew acronym for self-propelled heavy mortar
MAZKOM Rachav	Acronym for suspension and tracks, wide
MAZKOM Tzar	Acronym for suspension and tracks, narrow
moshav	collective agricultural settlement
Ro'em	'Thunderous', 155mm self-propelled howitzer on Sherman hull
sandalim	'Sandals', Hebrew slang for recoil wedges
Sayeret Netz	'Reconnaissance Hawk'
ta'oz	'strongholds', behind the Bar-Lev Line, along the 'Artillery Road'
TOMAT	Hebrew acronym for self-propelled gun
TZAHAL	Acronym for Tzva Hagana Le Yisrael = Israel Defence Force (IDF)
Tzidud Rachav	'Turning large' or wide turn, for re-positioning multiple vehicles
VVSS	Vertical Volute Spring Suspension (narrow tracks)
Yishuv	Literally 'settlement', refers to the area occupied by Jews, prior to modern Israel

APPENDICES

Sherman Designations		
American	British	Description
M4	Sherman I	75mm, VVSS, dry ammo stowage, 56-degree hull front, small hatch (IC= Firefly)
M4 Composite	Sherman I Hybrid	75mm, VVSS, dry ammo stowage, cast hull front, large hatch (initial small) (IC Hybrid= Firefly)
M4(105)	Sherman IB	105mm, VVSS, 47-degree hull front, large hatch
M4(105)HVSS	Sherman IBY	105mm, HVSS, 47-degree hull front, large hatch
M4A1	Sherman II	75mm, VVSS, dry ammo stowage, small hatch, later w/ large hatch, still dry ammo stowage
M4A1(76)	Sherman IIA	76mm, VVSS, wet ammo stowage, large hatch
M4A1(76)HVSS	Sherman IIAY	76mm, HVSS wet ammo stowage, large hatch
M4A2	Sherman III	75mm, VVSS, dry ammo stowage, later w/ 47-degree hull front, dry ammo stowage
M4A2(76)	Sherman IIIAY	76mm, HVSS, wet ammo stowage, 47-degree hull front
M4A3	Sherman IV	75mm, VVSS, small hatch, dry ammo stowage (M4A3 not used by British)
M4A3(76)	76mm, VVSS, wet ammo stowage, 47-degree hull front, large hatch	
M4A3(76)HVSS	76mm, HVSS, wet ammo stowage, 47-degree hull front, large hatch	
M4A3(105)	105mm, VVSS, 47-degree hull front, large hatch	
M4A3(105)HVSS	Same as above, except suspension	
M4A3E2	'Jumbo', assault tank w/ extra armour, wet ammo stowage, 75mm, w/some upgraded to 76mm	
M4A4	Sherman V	75mm, VVSS, dry ammo stowage, longer hull, 56-degree hull front, small hatch (VC = Firefly)
M4A6	75mm, VVSS, dry ammo stowage, cast hull front (M4A6 not used by British)	
Israeli		
M-3	Sherman with a 75mm Gun M3	
M-1	Sherman with a 76mm Gun M1, M1A1 or M1A2	
Super Sherman	M-1 Sherman with the HVSS suspension	
M-50	French 75mm gun CN-75-50 in round turret, all hull types, except M4A6	
M-51	French 105mm gun D1504 L44 in T23 style turret, large hatch, M4, M4A3, M4A1	

210

MEMORIALS

There are memorials all over Israel, to honor individuals, units and specific battles. The first M50 howitzer is in Elyachin, a town south of Hadera, in northern Israel. It is dedicated to Master Sergeant Shaked Ozeri, killed on May 4, 2000. He was the last IDF combat death before the final withdrawal from Lebanon. The howitzer is in pristine condition, as a memorial to a fallen soldier should be. Note the stowed firing pedestal and the mount for the training simulator on top. The second M50 howitzer is displayed in Kiryat Chaim, within the municipal limits of Haifa. (Osnat Rotlevi)

Preserved Items (Volume 1)	
Vehicle	**Location**
MACHMAT 160mm	*Beit Ha'Totchan* (Gunner's House or House of Artillerymen) near Zichron Ya'Akov, on the coast between Haifa (22.8 miles north) and Tel Aviv (43 miles south)
MACHMAT 160mm	*Yad La'Shiryon* (IDF Armored Corps Memorial & Museum), approx. 17 miles west of Jerusalem
MACHMAT 160mm (Test Vehicle)	*Batey Haosef* (IDF Collection Houses), in Tel Aviv-Yafo
L33 Ro'em	*Yad La'Shiryon*
L33 Ro'em	*Beit Ha'Totchan*
MAR240	*Yad La'Shiryon*
Episcopi (280mm rockets)	*Batey Haosef*
Episcopi (290mm rockets)	*Yad La'Shiryon*
Episcopi (290mm rockets)	*Beit Ha'Totchan*
240mm Truck-mounted Launcher	*Batey Haosef*
Sho't-based 290mm launcher	*Beit Ha'Totchan*
290mm Reload Truck	*Beit Ha'Totchan*
Keres (AGM-78 ARM on M809 5-Ton truck	Hatzerim Air Force Base, near Be'er Sheva, approximately 69 miles from Tel Aviv-Yafo
Kilshon	Hatzerim Air Force Base, near Be'er Sheva, approximately 69 miles from Tel Aviv-Yafo
Eyal Observation Post Tank	*Yad La'Shiryon*
Driver Training Tank	*Yad La'Shiryon*
Medical Evacuation Tank (test vehicle)	*Yad La'Shiryon*
Medical Evacuation Tank	*Yad La'Shiryon*
M10 Tank Destroyer	*Yad La'Shiryon*
M10 Tank Destroyer	*Batey Haosef*

Weapons	Location
Soltam 160mm mortar	*Beit Ha'Totchan & Batey Haosef*
M71 155mm howitzer	*Beit Ha'Totchan*

FURTHER READING

History of the IDF Artillery Corps

Israeli Sherman-based Self-Propelled Weapons

Volume 1

Tom Gannon

They called us...

The New Evil
Memories from Afghanistan 2006–2008

Warrant Officer (Ret'd) Marvin Craig MacNeill CD

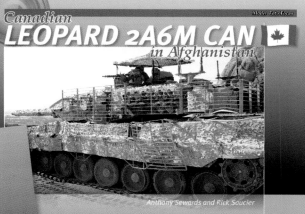

Model Foto Focus

Canadian
LEOPARD 2A6M CAN
in Afghanistan

Anthony Sewards and Rick Saucier

Trackpad Photo Album

IDF Jeeps

Tom Gannon

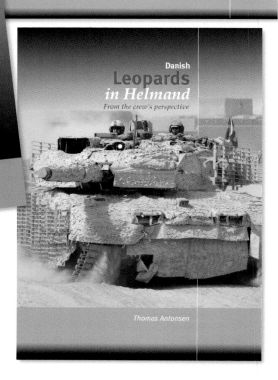

Danish
Leopards
in Helmand
From the crew's perspective

Thomas Antonsen

Available from

Trackpad 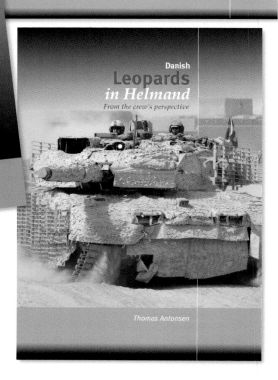 Publishing

Available from:
www.trackpadpublishing.com
www.facebook.com/trackpadpublishing
trackpadpublish@gmail.com

Published by Trackpad ▓▓ Publishing

18 Sandown Close
Blackwater
Camberley
Surrey
GU17 0EL
UK

www.trackpadpublishing.com
trackpadpublish@gmail.com

English copyright © Trackpad Publishing 2017
History of the IDF Artillery Corps
Israeli Sherman-based Self-Propelled Weapons, Volume 2
Tom Gannon
978-0-9928425-9-8

Designed and produced by Michael Shackleton

Printed by Scandinavian Book, c/o LaserTryk.co.uk Ltd. Hamilton House, Mabledon Place, Bloomsbury, WC1H 9BB

COMMENTS OR CORRECTIONS
While every effort has been made to ensure that the information contained herein is correct, some factual or typographical errors may be present. Should you detect an error, or simply wish to make a comment regarding this publication, please contact the publisher at any of the links above.